# PMP®
# Final Exam Review

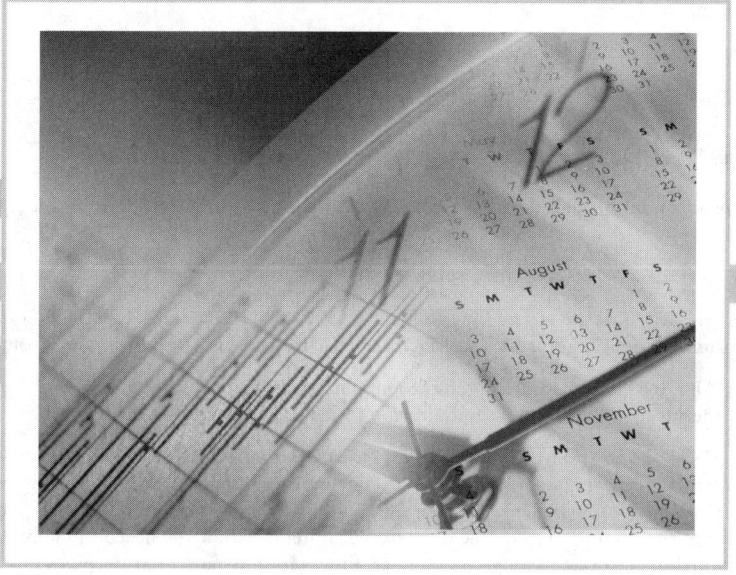

Kim Heldman, PMP

San Francisco • London

Associate Publisher: Neil Edde
Acquisitions Editor: Elizabeth Peterson
Developmental Editor: Heather O'Connor
Production Editor: Lori Newman
Technical Editor: Patti Jansen
Copyeditor: Sarah Lemaire
Compositor: Scott Benoit
CD Coordinator: Dan Mummert
CD Technician: Kevin Ly
Proofreaders: Laurie O'Connell, Nancy Riddiough
Book Designer: Bill Gibson, Judy Fung
Cover Design and Illustration: Richard Miller, Calyx Design
Cover Photographs: Getty Images, Duncan Smith, and Comstock Images

Copyright © 2004 SYBEX Inc., 1151 Marina Village Parkway, Alameda, CA 94501. World rights reserved. No part of this publication may be stored in a retrieval system, transmitted, or reproduced in any way, including but not limited to photocopy, photograph, magnetic, or other record, without the prior agreement and written permission of the publisher.

Library of Congress Card Number: 2003115679

ISBN: 0-7821-4324-5

SYBEX and the SYBEX logo are either registered trademarks or trademarks of SYBEX Inc. in the United States and/or other countries.

Screen reproductions produced with FullShot 99. FullShot 99 © 1991-1999 Inbit Incorporated. All rights reserved.

FullShot is a trademark of Inbit Incorporated.

The CD interface was created using Macromedia Director, COPYRIGHT 1994, 1997-1999 Macromedia Inc. For more information on Macromedia and Macromedia Director, visit http://www.macromedia.com.

TRADEMARKS: SYBEX has attempted throughout this book to distinguish proprietary trademarks from descriptive terms by following the capitalization style used by the manufacturer.

The author and publisher have made their best efforts to prepare this book, and the content is based upon final release software whenever possible. Portions of the manuscript may be based upon pre-release versions supplied by software manufacturer(s). The author and the publisher make no representation or warranties of any kind with regard to the completeness or accuracy of the contents herein and accept no liability of any kind including but not limited to performance, merchantability, fitness for any particular purpose, or any losses or damages of any kind caused or alleged to be caused directly or indirectly from this book.

Manufactured in the United States of America

10 9 8 7 6 5 4 3 2 1

## Software License Agreement: Terms and Conditions

The media and/or any online materials accompanying this book that are available now or in the future contain programs and/or text files (the "Software") to be used in connection with the book. SYBEX hereby grants to you a license to use the Software, subject to the terms that follow. Your purchase, acceptance, or use of the Software will constitute your acceptance of such terms.

The Software compilation is the property of SYBEX unless otherwise indicated and is protected by copyright to SYBEX or other copyright owner(s) as indicated in the media files (the "Owner(s)"). You are hereby granted a single-user license to use the Software for your personal, noncommercial use only. You may not reproduce, sell, distribute, publish, circulate, or commercially exploit the Software, or any portion thereof, without the written consent of SYBEX and the specific copyright owner(s) of any component software included on this media.

In the event that the Software or components include specific license requirements or end-user agreements, statements of condition, disclaimers, limitations or warranties ("End-User License"), those End-User Licenses supersede the terms and conditions herein as to that particular Software component. Your purchase, acceptance, or use of the Software will constitute your acceptance of such End-User Licenses.

By purchase, use or acceptance of the Software you further agree to comply with all export laws and regulations of the United States as such laws and regulations may exist from time to time.

### Software Support

Components of the supplemental Software and any offers associated with them may be supported by the specific Owner(s) of that material, but they are not supported by SYBEX. Information regarding any available support may be obtained from the Owner(s) using the information provided in the appropriate read.me files or listed elsewhere on the media.

Should the manufacturer(s) or other Owner(s) cease to offer support or decline to honor any offer, SYBEX bears no responsibility. This notice concerning support for the Software is provided for your information only. SYBEX is not the agent or principal of the Owner(s), and SYBEX is in no way responsible for providing any support for the Software, nor is it liable or responsible for any support provided, or not provided, by the Owner(s).

### Warranty

SYBEX warrants the enclosed media to be free of physical defects for a period of ninety (90) days after purchase. The Software is not available from SYBEX in any other form or media than that enclosed herein or posted to www.sybex.com. If you discover a defect in the media during this warranty period, you may obtain a replacement of identical format at no charge by sending the defective media, postage prepaid, with proof of purchase to:

SYBEX Inc.

Product Support Department

1151 Marina Village Parkway

Alameda, CA 94501

Web: http://www.sybex.com

After the 90-day period, you can obtain replacement media of identical format by sending us the defective disk, proof of purchase, and a check or money order for $10, payable to SYBEX.

### Disclaimer

SYBEX makes no warranty or representation, either expressed or implied, with respect to the Software or its contents, quality, performance, merchantability, or fitness for a particular purpose. In no event will SYBEX, its distributors, or dealers be liable to you or any other party for direct, indirect, special, incidental, consequential, or other damages arising out of the use of or inability to use the Software or its contents even if advised of the possibility of such damage. In the event that the Software includes an online update feature, SYBEX further disclaims any obligation to provide this feature for any specific duration other than the initial posting.

The exclusion of implied warranties is not permitted by some states. Therefore, the above exclusion may not apply to you. This warranty provides you with specific legal rights; there may be other rights that you may have that vary from state to state. The pricing of the book with the Software by SYBEX reflects the allocation of risk and limitations on liability contained in this agreement of Terms and Conditions.

### Shareware Distribution

This Software may contain various programs that are distributed as shareware. Copyright laws apply to both shareware and ordinary commercial software, and the copyright Owner(s) retains all rights. If you try a shareware program and continue using it, you are expected to register it. Individual programs differ on details of trial periods, registration, and payment. Please observe the requirements stated in appropriate files.

### Copy Protection

The Software in whole or in part may or may not be copy-protected or encrypted. However, in all cases, reselling or redistributing these files without authorization is expressly forbidden except as specifically provided for by the Owner(s) therein.

# Contents

*Introduction* ix

| | | | |
|---|---|---|---|
| **Chapter** | **1** | **PMP Final Exam Review 1** | **1** |
| **Chapter** | **2** | **PMP Final Exam Review 2** | **21** |
| **Chapter** | **3** | **PMP Final Exam Review 3** | **41** |
| **Chapter** | **4** | **PMP Final Exam Review 4** | **61** |
| **Chapter** | **5** | **Answers to Final Exam Reviews 1-4** | **81** |
| | | Answers to Final Exam Review 1 | 82 |
| | | Answers to Final Exam Review 2 | 90 |
| | | Answers to Final Exam Review 3 | 97 |
| | | Answers to Final Exam Review 4 | 104 |

# Introduction

Are you ready to take the Project Management Professional (PMP) exam sponsored by the Project Management Institute (PMI)? Here's your chance to test your knowledge of specific project management practices and *A Guide to the Project Management Body of Knowledge (PMBOK)* practices.

## Who Should Use This Book

This book is geared for candidates for the PMP exam who have prepared for the exam and want to be certain they have the knowledge and skills needed to answer PMI's tough questions. If you're anxious to see the types of questions PMI has in store for you, then this is the book for you.

Don't rely on studying the Bonus Exam questions from the *PMP: Final Exam Review* book exclusively as your study method. Be sure you:

- Understand the concepts behind the material presented in each exam objective.
- Memorize all the PMI formulas.
- Have a thorough understanding of the inputs, tools and techniques, and outputs of all the PMI processes, what their purposes are, and the process group they belong to.

If you're new to the PMP requirements and skills, I recommend you read *Project Management Jumpstart* and/or *PMP: Project Management Professional Study Guide, Second Edition*, both by Sybex, Inc. For further exploration of PMP skills, you might also consider reading the *PMP: Project Management Professional Workbook*.

## How to Use This Book and CD

I've devised four thorough and challenging practice exams for this book so you can enter the PMI exam with confidence. These same practice exams are available on the book's CD as well, so you can take the exams on paper or electronically. The CD contains mechanisms for objective-based tests allowing you to focus on specific elements of study like the Executing processes, for example. You can also be scored by objective, so you can determine those areas of the PMI exam topics where you need to focus your studying.

The CD that accompanies this book also contains over 200 thought-provoking flashcard questions that you can use to further your preparation for the exam.

## What Is the PMP Certification?

PMI was founded in 1969 and first started offering the Project Management Professional certification exam in 1984. PMI is accredited as an American National Standards Institute (ANSI) standards developer and also has the distinction of being the first organization to have their certification program attain International Organization for Standardization (ISO) 9001 recognition.

PMI boasts a worldwide membership of over 100,000, with members from 125 different countries. Local PMI chapters meet regularly and allow project managers to exchange information and learn about new tools and techniques of project management or new ways to use established techniques. I encourage you to join a local chapter and get to know other professionals in your field.

PMI is the leader in project management practices and is the most widely recognized organization and certification in the field. PMI strives to maintain and promote standards and ethics in this field and offers publications, training, seminars, chapters, special interest groups, and colleges to further the project management discipline.

## Why Become PMP Certified?

The following benefits are associated with becoming PMP certified:

- It demonstrates proof of professional achievement.
- It increases your marketability.
- It provides greater opportunity for advancement in your field.
- It raises customer confidence in you and your company's services.

## How to Become PMP Certified

There are several requirements you'll need to fulfill in order to sit for the PMP exam. PMI has detailed the certification process quite extensively at their website. Go to www.pmi.org and click the Professional Development and Careers tab to reveal the Certifications selection to get the latest information on certification procedures and requirements.

As of the date of this publication, you are required to fill out an application to sit for the PMP exam. You can submit this application online at http://certificationapp.pmi.org. You will also need to document 35 hours of formal project management education. This might include college classes, seminars, workshops, or training sessions. Be prepared to list the class titles, location, date, and content.

In addition to filling out the application and documenting your formal project management training, there is one additional set of criteria you'll need to meet to sit for the exam. These criteria fall into two categories. You need to meet the requirements for only one of these categories:

- Category 1 is for those who hold a baccalaureate degree. You'll need to provide proof, via transcripts, of your degree with your application. In addition, you'll need to complete verification forms—found at the PMI website—that show 4500 hours of project management experience that spans a minimum of three years and no more than six years.
- Category 2 is for those who do not hold a baccalaureate degree but do hold a high-school diploma or equivalent. You'll need to complete verification forms documenting 7500 hours of project management experience that spans a minimum of five years and no more than eight years.

The exam fee at the time of this publication is $405 for PMI members in good standing and $555 for non-PMI members. Testing is conducted at Prometric centers. You can find a center near you at the PMI website. You have six months from the time PMI receives and approves your completed application to take the exam. You'll need to bring a form of identification such as a driver's license with you to the Prometric center on the test day. You will not be allowed to take anything with you into the testing center. You will be given a calculator, pencils, and scrap paper by the center. You will turn in all scrap paper, including the notes and squiggles you've jotted during the test, to the center upon completion of the exam.

The exam is scored immediately, so you will know if you've passed at the conclusion of the test. You're given four hours to complete the exam, which consists of 200 randomly generated questions that cover the following process groups and areas: Initiation, Planning, Executing, Controlling, Closing, and Professional Responsibility. All unanswered questions are scored as wrong answers, so it benefits you to guess at an answer if you're stumped on a question.

After you've received your certification, you'll be required to earn 60 professional development units (PDUs) every three years to maintain certification. Approximately one hour of structured learning translates to one PDU. The PMI website details what activities constitute a PDU, how many PDUs each activity earns, and how to register your PDUs with PMI to maintain your certification. As an example, attendance at a local chapter meeting earns one PDU.

## Tips for Taking the PMP Exam

Here are some general tips for taking your exam successfully:

- Get to the exam center early so that you can relax and review your study materials.

- Read the exam questions very carefully. Make sure you know exactly what the question is asking and don't be tempted to answer too quickly.

- Unanswered questions score as wrong answers. It's better to guess than to leave a question unanswered.

- If you're not sure of an answer, use a process of elimination to identify the obvious incorrect answers first. Narrow the remaining choices down by referring back to the question, looking for key words that might tip you off to the correct answer.

- You'll be given scratch paper to take with you to the exam station. As soon as you get to your place, write down all the formulas and any other memory aids you used while studying before starting the exam. That way you can relax a little, because you won't have to remember the formulas when you get to those questions on the exam—you can simply look at your scratch paper.

- Visit the PMI website at www.pmi.org for the latest information regarding certification and to find a testing site nearest you.

# PMP Final Exam Review 1

1. 22 people are expected at your next stakeholder status meeting. Which of the following statements are true?

    A. There are 242 lines of communication.

    B. The number of attendees falls within the reasonable range for effective decision making.

    C. There are 231 lines of communication.

    D. There are too few people to make effective decisions.

2. You are a project manager for Katie's Kitchen. They market and sell homemade sauces to gourmet grocery store chains and upscale restaurants. Your project concerns adding two new machines to the production line. You have just finished calculating potential early start dates, early finish dates, late start dates, and late finish dates for your activities without regard to resource pool limitations. You've come up with the most likely estimate for each activity. All of the following statements are true except for which one? Choose the least correct answer.

    A. You've used CPM to calculate a single date for early start, early finish, late start, and late finish.

    B. You've performed mathematical analysis, which is a tool and technique of the Schedule Development process.

    C. Your next step might include duration compression followed by resource-leveling heuristics.

    D. You've created a project schedule but have not yet assigned resources.

3. If EV = 145, PV = 162, AC = 138, BAC = 200, and ETC = 62, what is EAC when you know past estimating assumptions are no longer valid?

    A. 190.4

    B. 193

    C. 201

    D. 200

4. You work in the pharmaceutical industry, and your organization is considering building a new laboratory facility in the Northwest. Market demand is driving new research for diet medications, and the new lab would be dedicated to this product development project. Some stakeholders in your organization are not certain a new lab facility is needed, because there is space that can be used in an existing building to host the diet medication research project. You've conducted a feasibility study, and the results show two possible ways to meet the space needs. Which of the following is true regarding this situation?

   A. Project selection methods are used by executive managers to determine things like public perception, financial return, customer loyalty, and so on, and are only used to choose among alternative projects.

   B. Project selection methods are a tool and technique of the Initiation process and can be used to choose among alternative ways of doing a project.

   C. Project selection methods are concerned with the type of things executive managers think about like public perception, financial return, customer loyalty, and so on.

   D. Project selection methods are an input to the Initiation process and can be used to choose among alternative ways of doing a project.

5. You work for a specialized book publisher that publishes 35 new titles per year. Your company has a specific process in place for managing each book project. They've found that managing most of the phases the same way across all the projects allows them to gain efficiencies they wouldn't get if they let each project manager use their own process. You're accepting your first assignment as the project manager over a new publication. You're responsible for seeing this project through from the beginning (assigning a qualified author to write on this topic) to the end (distributing the book to wholesalers and retailers). What does this scenario describe?

   A. Phase sequencing
   B. Progressive elaboration
   C. Organizational planning
   D. Program management

6. This tool and technique of Risk Monitoring and Control is interested in looking at the implementation and the effective use of the transference, avoidance, and mitigation risk strategies.

   A. Periodic project risk reviews
   B. Project change requests
   C. Project risk response audit
   D. Workaround plans

7. Organizing resource pools, assisting with cost estimating, information retrieval, and creating network diagrams are all examples of attributes of this tool and technique. Choose the best answer.
   A. Expert judgment
   B. Spreadsheet programs
   C. Project management software
   D. Templates

8. You're the project manager for Dream Clinics, a research organization that specializes in sleep disorders. You're working on an internal service project and are in the beginning of the Planning processes. You noticed that specific staff members were named as project team members during your review of the project charter. Which of the following does this question describe?
   A. Resource requirements, which are an output of Resource Planning
   B. Preassignment, which is a tool and technique of Staff Acquisition
   C. Staffing requirements, which are an input to Organizational Planning
   D. Resource pool description, which is an input to Resource Planning

9. The risk management plan accomplishes all of the following except:
   A. The risk management plan describes how risk identification will be structured and performed during the project.
   B. The risk management plan describes how qualitative and quantitative analysis will be structured and performed during the project.
   C. The risk management plan addresses risk response planning and how it will be carried out during the project.
   D. The risk management plan addresses responses to individual risks and how they will be carried out during the project.

10. Your project sponsor has asked you for a forecast of the likely total cost of the project based on performance to date. Which of the following statements is true?
    A. You'll use the EAC calculation, which is an output of the Cost Control process.
    B. You'll use the EAC calculation, which is an output of the Performance Reporting process.
    C. You'll use the ETC calculation, which is an output of the Cost Control process.
    D. You'll use the ETC calculation, which is an output of the Performance Reporting process.

11. You are using the interviewing technique of the Quantitative Risk Analysis process. The probability distribution you intend to use is triangular distribution. All of the following statements are true regarding this question except:

    A. Interviewing techniques are used to quantify the probability and impact of the risks on project objectives.

    B. The information gathered depends on the type of probability distribution used.

    C. This process typically uses continuous probability distributions.

    D. Triangular distributions rely on mean and standard deviation to quantify risks.

12. You are contracting services for your current project. You need three chemical engineers with specific skills (outlined in the statement of work) to work on your project. You've decided to prepare an RFQ because your organization is basing their source selection decision on which of the following? Choose the best answer.

    A. Subject matter expertise

    B. A fixed price contract

    C. Technical skills

    D. Price

13. If EV = 114, PV = 120, and AC = 103, what are CPI and SPI, respectively? (Answers are rounded to the highest decimal.)

    A. 1.1 and .95

    B. 1.2 and 1.05

    C. 1.05 and 1.2

    D. .95 and 1.1

14. You're a project manager for Music On Demand Internet Services, and you're in the Risk Monitoring and Control process. Your project, when completed, will provide a way for any Internet user to purchase music on demand from the recording company you work for. Your testers are testing the download process now but discover that the name of the song and other textual information does not download properly. What is this an example of?

    A. Technical performance measurement

    B. Workaround

    C. Periodic project risk reviews

    D. Corrective action

15. You're in the midst of managing a project for the water and sanitation district of your local city. It's a large, complicated project that you've divided into smaller, manageable projects with their own project managers who all report to you. Two of these projects have been contracted out to a vendor. You know that specific technical elements must be adhered to in the design and implementation of this project due to regulations governing the water and sanitation district. Two other project managers in the district are busy working on unrelated projects, but they're subject to the same regulations and processes as your project. These regulations won't affect your next project, which you've learned is with the city police department. Which of the following statements is *not* true?

    A. The water and sanitation district prefers managing their projects in a coordinated fashion known as programs.

    B. Phase exits are required for all vendor projects.

    C. The projects in this district are considered an application area due to their common elements.

    D. Your project is employing the use of subprojects.

16. These two processes in the Controlling process group are performed in parallel to assure correctness and acceptance of the work. Which two processes are concerned with correctness and acceptance, respectively?

    A. Quality Assurance and Scope Change Control

    B. Scope Verification and Quality Control

    C. Quality Control and Scope Verification

    D. Scope Change Control and Quality Assurance

17. All of the following statements are true regarding the time constraints of imposed dates and key events except:

    A. Imposed dates and key events constraints are an input to the Project Plan Development process.

    B. Imposed dates apply to activities that must start no later than or finish no later than a specific date.

    C. The key events time constraint applies to the completion of deliverables by the requested date of a stakeholder.

    D. Requested completion dates often become expected dates and therefore pose a time constraint.

18. You are a project manager working on contract for a farming cooperative. They've decided to introduce six new wild juice drinks to the market that mix combinations of exotic juices to create some new exciting flavors. You've performed a feasibility study to determine the best way to go about producing, manufacturing, and marketing the wild juice drinks. Your research has yielded three alternatives that you want to compare based on today's value. The project's initial investment is $29,000. Alternative A's cash flows are $14,000 for year 1 and $19,000 for year 2. Alternative B's cash inflows are $21,000 for year 1 and $20,000 for year 2. Alternative C's cash inflows are $15,000 for year 1 and $20,000 for year 2. Assume a 10 percent cost of capital. Which project should you recommend?

    A. Alternative C
    B. Alternative B
    C. Alternative A
    D. Alternative B and C are both acceptable.

19. All of the following Controlling processes have a change control system as a tool and technique of the process except:

    A. Quality Control
    B. Scope Change Control
    C. Schedule Control
    D. Cost Control

20. Which of the following is true regarding constraints?

    A. Projects that are subject to the triple constraints do not usually have any other constraints.
    B. The triple constraints are time, quality, and capital.
    C. The triple constraints will most likely affect all projects, with one or two constraints being the primary driver of the project.
    D. Projects that are subject to the triple constraints are more easily managed within a functional organization than within a weak matrix organization.

21. You are working on a project that is similar in scope to a project performed last year by your company. You might consider which of the following?

    A. Using the previous project's alternatives identification as a template
    B. Reusing the previous project's benefit/cost analysis as justification for this project
    C. Using the previous project's WBS as a template
    D. Reusing the previous project's product description when writing the scope statement

**22.** You and your friend are studying together for the PMP exam. You purchased a copy of this book to study from while your friend purchased a copy of another author's book. Both books came with a CD. You each decide to copy the CD from the book you purchased to share with each other. Which of the following statements is true? Choose the best answer.

   **A.** Since neither of you is a PMP yet, you're not required to adhere to the *PMP Code of Professional Conduct*, so sharing the CDs is acceptable.

   **B.** You and your friend should not share the CDs because of conflict of interest.

   **C.** The CDs with both books are considered intellectual property and should not be copied.

   **D.** You and your friend should not share the CDs because of the appearance of impropriety.

**23.** You are the project manager for Changing Tides video games. You have gathered the inputs for the Activity Duration Estimating process. Which of the following tools and techniques will you employ to produce the outputs for this process?

   **A.** Activity list, analogous estimating, qualitatively based durations, and alternatives identification

   **B.** Activity list, analogous estimating, expert judgment, and qualitatively based durations

   **C.** Expert judgment, analogous estimating, quantitatively based durations, and reserve time

   **D.** Expert judgment, alternatives identification, quantitatively based durations, and reserve time

**24.** Which of the following is *not* a major step of decomposition?

   **A.** Identify major deliverables.

   **B.** Identify constituent components.

   **C.** Determine adequate cost, schedule, resource, and quality estimates.

   **D.** Verify correctness of decomposition.

**25.** You have received three estimates for your project activity. The optimistic estimate is 245 days, the pessimistic estimate is 269 days, and the most likely estimate is 257 days. This particular activity is critical to the project, and your project sponsor wants to know with 95 percent certainty how long it will take to complete this activity. Which of the following do you tell the project sponsor? (The answers are rounded to the nearest whole number.)

   **A.** 265 days to 273 days

   **B.** 253 days to 261 days

   **C.** 261 days to 277 days

   **D.** 249 days to 265 days

**26.** The risk management team is ready to assess the probability of the risks occurring and their potential effects on the project objectives. The team has decided to use a PI matrix to assign risk ratings. Which of the following statements is true?

   **A.** The PI matrix can be developed using cardinal or ordinal scales.

   **B.** The scales of probability determine the potential effect a risk has on the project objectives and are used as an input to the PI calculation.

   **C.** The PI matrix is a tool and technique of the Risk Identification process.

   **D.** Risk impact scales are an input to the PI calculation and are always made up of cardinal values.

**27.** You are working on an estimate for overall project duration. All of the following statements are true except:

   **A.** Activity Duration Estimating tools and techniques can be used to estimate overall project duration.

   **B.** Schedule Development is the most appropriate process to use to determine overall project duration.

   **C.** You could use expert judgment, analogous estimating, quantitatively based durations, or reserve time (contingency) to estimate overall project duration.

   **D.** You could use a schedule change control system, performance measurement, additional planning, project management software, or variance analysis to estimate overall project duration.

**28.** This process is where activities are clarified, the work of the project is authorized to begin, and resources are committed and then carry out their assigned activities to create the product or service of the project. Which process does this describe?

   **A.** Project Plan Development

   **B.** Project Plan Execution

   **C.** Schedule Development

   **D.** Team Development

29. You are a project manager working on contract. The organization that's contracted with your company is not happy with the progress of the project to date. They claim that an important deliverable was overlooked and that you should halt the project and reassess how to meet this deliverable. You know that the customer has approved all phases of the project to date. Which of the following statements is true?

   A. You and your company may have to use problem-solving techniques such as arbitration and mediation to reach an agreement.

   B. You and your company may have to use communication techniques such as arbitration and mediation to reach an agreement.

   C. You and your company may have to use negotiation techniques such as arbitration and mediation to reach an agreement.

   D. You and your company may have to use influencing techniques such as arbitration and mediation to reach an agreement.

30. You are working late into the evening with the project team to finish a deliverable and meet the scheduled completion date. The team closes in on completion when an error is discovered. Fixing the error will actually cause a change in scope. You know that scope changes require approval of the CCB, but if you don't give the team the go-ahead to fix this error, this deliverable will be late. Which of the following actions do you take? Choose the best answer.

   A. All scope changes require approval of the CCB. You inform your team to stop working until you can get the CCB to approve or deny the change.

   B. The change control system gives you the authority to approve emergency changes. Since this is an emergency and your authority to approve the decision is documented, you decide to tell the team to fix the error.

   C. The change control system documents the procedures for approving change requests. Since there are no procedures documented in your change control system for emergencies, you inform the team to stop working until you can get the CCB to approve or deny the change.

   D. The change control system documents the procedures for approving change requests. There are no procedures documented in your change control system for emergencies. But you know that time is the primary constraint for this project, so you decide to approve the change yourself and tell the team to fix the error. You will inform the CCB at the next meeting of the change.

31. You are a project manager working on contract for a farming cooperative. They've decided to introduce six new wild juice drinks to the market that mix combinations of exotic juices to create some new exciting flavors. You've performed a feasibility study to determine the best way to go about producing, manufacturing, and marketing the wild juice drinks. Your research has yielded three alternatives that you want to compare based on today's value. The project's initial investment is $94,000. The total present value of Alternative A's cash inflows is $95,120. The total present value of Alternative B's cash inflows is $93,889. The total present value of Alternative C's cash inflows is $94,243. Assume a 10 percent cost of capital. Which project should you recommend?
    A. Alternative A and B are both acceptable.
    B. Alternative B
    C. Alternative A and C are both acceptable.
    D. Alternative B and C are both acceptable.

32. The project management processes together constitute which of the following?
    A. Deliverables
    B. Fast tracking
    C. Project life cycle
    D. Project management

33. All of the following statements are true regarding quality improvements except:
    A. Quality improvements might reveal ways to improve efficiency or effectiveness on the project, with an end result of exceeding stakeholder expectations.
    B. Quality improvements come about as a result of quality audits.
    C. Quality improvements help identify lessons learned to improve efficiency or effectiveness on future projects.
    D. Quality improvements are implemented as a result of change requests or corrective actions.

34. You are a project manager for Basement Refinishers, Inc. You've taken on a new project that requires demolition of the existing basement walls, wiring, and plumbing before new construction can start. The new design plan is completed, and the homeowners have signed off. The demolition activity is an example of which of the following?
    A. Hard logic
    B. Preferential logic
    C. Soft logic
    D. Manual logic

35. One of your project's deliverables requires skills in journalism. You have three resources working on the activities that need to be completed for this deliverable. One of the resources accidentally discovers that the other two journalists are making a salary that's significantly more than their salary. Which of the following statements is true?

    A. The Hygiene Theory says salary isn't a motivator unless there are large disparities in salary.

    B. Maslow contends that salary is a self-esteem need.

    C. The Expectancy Theory says that salary isn't a motivator regardless of pay discrepancies.

    D. The Achievement Theory contends that salary is tied to achievement, so that large disparities in salary become a demotivator.

36. You work for Star Bank as a project manager. Your project is so large and risky that you're not certain the organization should undertake it. You propose conducting a feasibility study, as its own project, to examine the benefits of the new proposed project. The feasibility study is approved and begun. Which of the following statements is *not* true regarding this project?

    A. The Initiation process occurs at the beginning of the project, when chances for a successful completion are high and the staffing levels are low.

    B. The Initiation process acknowledges that the next project phase should begin. Costs are low in this process, while the risks are high.

    C. The Initiation process is where approval is granted to undertake the project and the organization's resources are authorized to begin work.

    D. The Initiation process acknowledges that the next project phase should begin. The stakeholders have the most influence over the product or service of the project during this process.

37. You and a friend of yours have started your own consulting firm. Both of you are PMPs. You've given an estimate to a prospective client to manage a project they're starting up next month. This is an important job, and this client would be an excellent reference for you if things go well. You know all of the following statements are true except:

    A. Your estimate of costs should accurately reflect the services you're going to provide.

    B. If you get the job, you should stick to the scope and objectives you outlined in your bid or contract regarding the professional services you'll render.

    C. You should respect the confidentiality of the information you'll come across during the course of this project.

    D. Since it's close to the holiday season, you send an expensive gift basket to the client in the hopes they'll pick your company to run this project.

**38.** Parametric modeling is most reliable when all of the following conditions are met except for which one? Choose the least accurate answer.

   **A.** The model is scalable.

   **B.** The parameters used are easily quantifiable.

   **C.** The resources preparing the estimates have the needed expertise.

   **D.** Any historical information used is accurate.

**39.** You've decided to branch out into project management consulting and have landed your first contracting assignment. You are working on an exciting project for a small company that provides pet-sitting services in people's homes. The employee who is the designated project manager on this project doesn't have much experience running projects. He insists that the Activity Sequencing process must be completed as its own separate process and cannot be combined with the Activity Duration Estimating process. You assure him that it is an acceptable step to take. Which of the following best describes your answer to his concern?

   **A.** Project Time Management allows for completing the Activity Sequencing, Activity Duration Estimating, and Schedule Control processes as one process. On a project this small, all these processes can be completed at one time by one person.

   **B.** Project Integration Management allows for completing the Activity Sequencing, Activity Duration Estimating, and Schedule Development processes as one process. On a project this small, all these processes can be completed at one time by one person.

   **C.** Project Integration Management allows for completing the Activity Sequencing, Activity Duration Estimating, and Schedule Control processes as one process. On a project this small, all these processes can be completed at one time by one person.

   **D.** Project Time Management allows for completing the Activity Sequencing, Activity Duration Estimating, and Schedule Development processes as one process. On a project this small, all these processes can be completed at one time by one person.

**40.** Your project selection committee is meeting later this week and is considering initiating one of two projects. They've asked you to recommend the project that will benefit the organization the most. The information you've gathered shows the initial investment for Project 1 is $295,000. Monthly cash inflows for the first year are $17,000, and expected cash inflows beginning in year 2 are $36,000 per quarter. Project 2 has an initial investment of $332,000. Expected quarterly inflows for the first year are $44,000. Beginning in the second year, inflows are expected to be $12,000 monthly. Which project should you recommend to the committee and why?

   **A.** Project 1, because it has a payback period of 20 months, which is shorter than Project 2's payback period.

   **B.** Project 1, because it has a payback period of 23 months, while Project 2 has a payback period of 28 months.

   **C.** Project 1, because it has a lower initial investment than Project 2.

   **D.** Project 1, because it has a payback period of 16 months, while Project 2 has a payback period of 21 months.

**41.** This part of the risk management plan describes how the project management team will measure its effectiveness at executing risk responses.

   A. Methodology
   B. Thresholds
   C. Tracking
   D. Timing

**42.** You have just taken over the project management duties for a large, complex project from a project manager who is retiring. The first thing you do is review the project charter, then the scope statement, followed by the work breakdown structure (WBS). The work package level of the WBS appears to be deliverables. You need to understand what the work at this level entails for each work package and which department or vendor has been assigned to each work package. Which of the following places will you look to determine this information?

   A. The procurement management plan
   B. The scope statement
   C. The WBS dictionary
   D. The project charter

**43.** You are performing some of the processes in the Project Cost Management knowledge area. Which of the following statements is *not* true?

   A. Value Engineering is a technique that considers a group of costs collectively when deciding among competing alternatives.
   B. Financial analysis is sometimes required to help predict project performance.
   C. This knowledge area is primarily concerned with the cost of resources.
   D. Resource Planning is one of the processes in this knowledge area.

**44.** You are the director of the project management office (PMO) for your organization. Terri, an employee from another department, has approached you about a new project that is being talked about in her department. Terri would like the opportunity to head up this project and wants to convince you of her knowledge of project management and that she can do this job. The project will convert all distribution centers in the USA to Radio Frequency Identification (RFID) tags. This new technology will improve inventory management by giving management a real-time view of demand for the products they sell. It will also help reduce theft and reduce stock-outs. You have already had a meeting with the CEO regarding this project and have a good feeling this project will likely get approved. You tell her all of the following except which one?

   A. Terri should write a project overview, so that the executive management team and the project sponsor can understand the intended outcome of the project and see an initial list of the key deliverables to know what they're getting.
   B. This project may get outsourced to a vendor. If that's the case, you'll be utilizing the processes in the Project Procurement Management knowledge area that are considered from the perspective of the vendor.
   C. Terri should make certain the deliverables are measurable.
   D. Terri should make certain the goals are measurable.

**45.** You have been with your company for three months. You were hired as a project manager and are anxious to get started on your first project. Your organization is considering taking on a project that has considerable risk associated with it. You've written the project overview, defined the goals, and identified the key deliverables for the executive team to review and evaluate. The committee is meeting two weeks from today to decide on this project. Since you're new to the company, you want to make a good impression. The Initiation phase of this project is just beginning, so you do which of the following?

   **A.** You make certain that the product description is documented, the strategic plan is considered, project selection criteria is determined, and historical information is considered before the committee meets.

   **B.** You make certain to pass on the information you've gathered and documented to the project sponsor, so that she can write the project charter prior to the evaluation committee meeting.

   **C.** You know some of the deliverables in this project will be purchased. You will use EVM techniques to help optimize life-cycle costs when you get to the processes in the Project Cost Management knowledge area.

   **D.** You know quality is the primary constraint on this project. When you get to the Project Quality Management knowledge area, processes will focus on the quality of the end product of the project exclusively.

**46.** You are a project manager for Lightening Bolt Enterprises. Your new project involves the research and development of a new type of rechargeable battery. The project objectives, as documented in the scope statement, should include which of the following?

   **A.** A description of the business need that brought about this project

   **B.** A brief summary of the product description, including measurable, quantifiable product requirements that will help measure project success

   **C.** Quantifiable criteria, including at least cost, schedule, and quality measures

   **D.** Quantifiable criteria derived from value engineering, value analysis, or function analysis

**47.** Your project is progressing nicely. One of the key deliverables for your project was contracted out to a vendor, but your organization is performing all the remaining work of the project. The completion of this deliverable marks the end of the design phase of the project. There are two project phases remaining. Which of the following Closing processes should be performed, if any?

   **A.** Contract Closeout and Administrative Closure

   **B.** Administrative Closure only

   **C.** Contract Closeout only

   **D.** No closing processes should be performed yet, because the work of the project isn't finished.

**48.** You work in the pharmaceutical industry, and your organization is considering building a new laboratory facility in the Northwest. Market demand is driving new research for diet medications, and the new lab would be dedicated to this product development project. Which of the following options is *not* true regarding the initiation of this project?

   **A.** Your selection committee has asked you to conduct a study that will determine if a new laboratory facility is necessary or if the unused space in the existing lab can be put to use for this project. A determination to initiate the project will not be made until this analysis is complete. Once initiation is approved, a formal link between the lab project and the ongoing work of the organization will be established.

   **B.** Some organizations—yours is one of them—require a limited amount of work or analysis before approvals are given for formal initiation. This is especially true for new product development projects and internal service projects.

   **C.** Initiation of the project cannot occur until the project selection criteria methods have outlined and determined the value or benefits of the project to the project owner. This won't be known until you conduct a feasibility study or needs analysis.

   **D.** Your selection committee has asked you to conduct a feasibility study to determine the needs of the new lab facility. When the feasibility study is completed and the project is approved for initiation, you plan on using the expert judgment tool and technique to examine the product description, strategic plan, project selection criteria, and historical information to choose among alternative methods of conducting this project.

**49.** Your project selection committee is evaluating three projects. They are using a weighted scoring model that has three criteria: decrease training time, streamline customer support functions, and return on investment. The weights for each of these criteria are 5, 4, and 2 respectively. Your selection committee has finished scoring the three projects and has given you the scores for the three criteria. They are as follows:

   Project 1: decrease training = 5, streamline support = 3, return on investment = 5

   Project 2: decrease training = 3, streamline support = 5, return on investment = 5

   Project 3: decrease training = 4, streamline support = 4, return on investment = 3

   Which project should you choose based on the scores from the weighted scoring model?

   **A.** Project 3
   **B.** Project 2
   **C.** Project 1
   **D.** There isn't enough information in the question to determine an answer.

**50.** Now that the Planning processes are over and your team is thick into the work of the project, you've kicked your feet up to take a breather. You no sooner get your right leg planted on the desk when one of your team members pops their head in your door. One of your project deliverables is in trouble. The schedule completion date is approaching, and this team member tells you that a risk trigger has surfaced. You need to take immediate action to reduce the probability of negative consequences occurring to the project as a result of this risk event. You might choose do to all of the following tasks except which one? Choose the least correct answer.

  **A.** Engage in preventive action.

  **B.** Put the contingency plan for this risk event into place.

  **C.** Engage in corrective action.

  **D.** Report the risk trigger and the actions you took at the next stakeholder status meeting.

**51.** You have just passed the PMP exam. Your friend is still studying and plans on taking the exam next month. You purchased a copy of this book to study from, while your friend purchased a copy of another author's book. Since you're finished studying, you agree to loan your book with the CD to your friend so she can use it to study from also. Which of the following statements is true? Choose the best answer.

  **A.** Since you are a PMP, you're required to adhere to the *PMP Code of Professional Conduct*, so sharing the book and CD is not acceptable.

  **B.** Since you are a PMP, you should not share the book and CD with your friend, because it may pose a conflict of interest for your friend.

  **C.** The book and CD are considered intellectual property and should not be copied. However, loaning your copy to your friend to use, as long as she doesn't copy it, is acceptable.

  **D.** Since you are a PMP, you're required to adhere to the *PMP Code of Professional Conduct* and should not share the book and CD with your friend because of the appearance of impropriety.

**52.** You are heading up the annual holiday party project for your organization and are working on the Organizational Planning process. You report to the director of human resources. You send an e-mail request to the marketing department asking for one full-time resource to research and hire entertainment for the party (including the children's activities). However, there is a lot of contention regarding this project because the marketing department headed it up last year. The director of marketing responds to you with an e-mail stating you should stop working on the project, because she's appointing someone from her own organization to head this up. All of the following statements are true regarding this question except for which one?

  **A.** The organizational structure has a large impact on project communications.

  **B.** Formal and informal reporting relationships should be considered when documenting roles and responsibilities.

  **C.** You were attempting to determine what resources were required and how many were needed when the marketing manager changed project managers.

  **D.** You work in a functional organization, which is a constraint of this project.

53. All of the following statements are true regarding Quality Planning except:
    A. Quality Planning involves identifying the quality standards for the project and devising a plan to meet them.
    B. The primary cost of meeting quality requirements is the expenses incurred while using the tools and techniques of this process.
    C. Quality is planned in, not inspected in.
    D. The tools and techniques of the Quality Planning process are the most often used quality tools and techniques on projects.

54. What are the outputs of the Risk Identification process?
    A. Risks, triggers, and inputs to other processes
    B. Risks, triggers, secondary risks, and inputs to other processes
    C. List of prioritized risks, triggers, and inputs to other processes
    D. List of prioritized risks, residual risks, secondary risks, triggers, and inputs to other processes

55. All of the following are true statements regarding the Quantitative Risk Analysis process except for which one?
    A. This process uses techniques like Monte Carlo analysis, which is a type of sensitivity analysis.
    B. This process determines the size of the schedule and cost contingency reserves.
    C. This process helps determine the probability of achieving the project objectives.
    D. This process generally follows Qualitative Risk Analysis but can be performed separately if desired.

56. Estimates to complete one of your project activities have been turned into you from experts on your project team. The estimates are as follows: The pessimistic estimate is 126 days, the optimistic estimate is 108 days, and the most likely estimate is 114 days. You can say with 68 percent certainty that the project will finish within which range of dates? (The answers are rounded to the nearest whole number.)
    A. 112 days to 118 days
    B. 111 days to 117 days
    C. 114 days to 116 days
    D. 113 days to 115 days

**57.** The expected value for your project duration estimate is 627 days, and the most likely duration estimate is 575. The standard deviation is 14. Which of the following statements is true?

   **A.** A 95 percent confidence factor would make this project duration between 547 days and 603 days.

   **B.** The project duration—given a 95 percent confidence factor—is between 613 days and 641 days.

   **C.** The project duration—given a 99 percent confidence factor—is between 585 days and 669 days.

   **D.** A 68 percent confidence factor would make this project duration between 547 days and 603 days.

**58.** All of the following statements are true regarding the Team Development process except for which one? Choose the least correct answer.

   **A.** The outputs of the Team Development process are performance improvements and input to performance appraisals.

   **B.** Team Development is performed during the Executing processes.

   **C.** Team building activities include both management actions and individual actions to improve team performance.

   **D.** Collocation is a technique used to help the team perform better.

**59.** One of your project's deliverables requires skills in journalism. You have three resources working on the activities that need to be completed for this deliverable. One of the resources accidentally discovers that the other two journalists are making a salary that's significantly more than their salary. As soon as this situation is brought to your attention, you correct it and bring this team member's salary in line with the other two journalists. Which of the following statements is true? Choose the best answer.

   **A.** Salary is a motivator because, according to Herzberg, the inequality in pay is a hygiene factor.

   **B.** Salary is no longer a motivator, because the need has been fulfilled.

   **C.** This team member's need has been fulfilled and now, according to Maslow, the ability to advance, the opportunity to learn new things, and the challenges involved in the work become motivators.

   **D.** The Expectancy Theory says that the importance of camaraderie with other team members is an important motivator.

**60.** This win-win conflict resolution technique is the one that project managers should use most.

   **A.** Confrontation

   **B.** Compromise

   **C.** Withdrawal

   **D.** Smoothing

**61.** Modifications to deliverables, product changes, and termination for poor performance are all examples of which of the following? Choose the best answer.

   **A.** They are factors that might generate change requests, which are an input to the Contract Administration process.

   **B.** They are a result of monitoring work requests, which are an output of the Contract Administration process.

   **C.** They are results of performance reports, which are a tool and technique of the Contract Administration process.

   **D.** They are factors that might generate seller invoices, which are a tool and technique of the Contract Administration process.

**62.** This tool and technique of the Cost Control process continuously monitors and measures what three elements?

   **A.** EVM measures CP, CPI, and EAC.

   **B.** EV measures AC, CV, and ETC.

   **C.** EVM measures PV, EV, and AC.

   **D.** EV measures EV, AC, and EAC.

**63.** You are a project manager working on a new ad campaign for the holiday season. Part of this project entails a series of new TV commercials. You contracted out the production of the commercials that will air during the busy buying season. Now all of the work of the project is done, and you're in the process of closing out the project. You're gathering information from team members and the vendor—including the scripts for the commercials that your project team developed—to archive. Which of the following options contains this information, given the circumstances in this question? Choose the best answer.

   **A.** Administrative documentation

   **B.** Product documentation

   **C.** Contract documentation

   **D.** Other project records

**64.** Which of the following statements does *not* pertain to the Scope Planning process?

   **A.** Scope Planning is the first core process in the Planning process group.

   **B.** The scope statement, an output of Scope Planning, identifies both the project objectives and project deliverables.

   **C.** Supporting detail for the scope statement—both of which are outputs of this process—should be documented, because you'll refer to this information in other processes.

   **D.** Two of the Scope Planning inputs are product description and historical information, and two tools and techniques are benefits/cost analysis and expert judgment.

# PMP Final Exam Review 2

1. All of the following statements are true regarding the Closing processes except:
   A. Contract Closeout is part of the Project Procurement Management knowledge area.
   B. Administrative Closure is part of the Project Procurement Management knowledge area.
   C. Contract Closeout verifies that the work of the project was completed accurately and satisfactorily.
   D. Administrative Closure does not have to verify the work of the project if the Contract Closeout process was performed.

2. Which of the following statements is *not* true regarding the work breakdown structure (WBS)?
   A. Like the scope statement, WBS is used as a common understanding of project scope.
   B. Like the decomposition process, each level in the WBS is generally assigned a unique identifier.
   C. Like the scope statement, work not shown on the WBS is not work of the project.
   D. Like the decomposition process, each level of the WBS should show an increasing level of detail that describes the project deliverables.

3. You are a project manager for Fountain of Youth Spring Water bottlers. You are installing a new accounting system and have identified several problems and their causes. You decide to use which of the following to identify the variables that will have the greatest effect on project outcomes?
   A. Design of experiments
   B. Benchmarking
   C. Benefit/cost analysis
   D. Flowcharting

4. One of your team members, a fellow PMP, is under investigation for violation of the *PMP Code of Professional Conduct*. What action should you take?
   A. Cooperate fully with PMI in the investigation.
   B. Tell PMI it would be a conflict of interest for you to cooperate in the investigation, because this person is your team member.
   C. Tell PMI it would be a conflict of interest for you to cooperate, because they may uncover information about you during the investigation that could cause them to investigate you.
   D. Cooperate with PMI by truthfully answering all their questions but refuse to give them any written documentation.

5. Your project is a multi-million dollar project and is one of the largest projects your organization has ever undertaken. You are in the Executing process and according to the project schedule, it's time to order equipment for a major deliverable no later than the end of this week. Since you have a free moment, you pick up the phone and give the heads-up to the procurement department to order your equipment. To your dismay, you're told that the proper paperwork hasn't been filled out, and once they get that, they'll need approval from the project sponsor. Which of the following statements is true regarding this question? Choose the best answer.

   A. This is a risk trigger and requires you to implement the mitigation strategy immediately.

   B. This problem will likely cause a variance in the project schedule that will require earned value analysis and corrective action to get the project work lined up with the schedule.

   C. This problem requires both preventative and corrective action.

   D. This is an organizational procedure that should have been taken into consideration during this process to avoid schedule delays.

6. You are a project manager working on an electronics project. Some of the deliverables that are needed to complete a prototype will require testing. The testing activity has two branches: pass and fail. If the deliverable fails the test, correction will be made and the test will be repeated. What is the best way to diagram these activities?

   A. Arrow diagramming method

   B. Precedence diagramming method

   C. Conditional diagramming method

   D. Network diagramming method

7. Your company manufactures a line of upscale body lotions. Your assignment entails designing a new line of after-shave lotion. This is a critical project for your company, and you've been given full authority to manage it. Your project team will consist of team members from several functional areas. The VP of Sales has managed projects of this nature in the past and will be actively involved in this project and the critical decision-making process. Your boss, the VP of Marketing, has the authority to assign resources to this project, and she is the go-to person for all critical project decisions. Given these statements, which of the following is *not* true?

   A. The VP of Sales is the project sponsor.

   B. This is a composite organization.

   C. Your boss is a stakeholder.

   D. This project's success relies on meeting the stated goals and objectives of the project and satisfactorily meeting or exceeding the expectations of your boss and the VP of Sales.

8. Your quality assurance team has discovered several problems with the product of your project. They've ordered the problems by frequency of occurrence on a diagram and have determined that roughly 80 percent of the problems are occurring due to 20 percent of the causes they've identified. All of the following statements are true except:

   A. You should spend the majority of your effort on the causes that are generating 80 percent of the problems.
   B. The 80/20 rule was first observed by Crosby.
   C. This is a tool and technique of the Quality Control process.
   D. This type of diagram is a histogram.

9. Benefit measurement methods and constrained optimization methods are also known as which of the following?

   A. EVM
   B. Mandatory dependencies
   C. Decision models
   D. Screening systems

10. All of the following statements are true regarding communication except:

    A. Communication involves a sender, message, and receiver.
    B. Communication occupies 80 percent of a project manager's time.
    C. Communication might be written or verbal (and includes formal and informal formats).
    D. Communication is one of the most important skills a project manager can master.

11. During this contract life cycle phase, the project objectives are refined and confirmed. A review of the potential qualified vendors takes place and solicitation materials such as the RFP are prepared. What contract life cycle phase is this?

    A. Selection
    B. Solicitation
    C. Requisition
    D. Award

12. You are a project manager working for a television film production company. Your organization practices phase sequencing and requires reviews and approvals of each phase before the next phase can begin. What is this process called?

    A. Stage gate
    B. Phase review
    C. Gate review
    D. Phase point

13. When negotiating with functional managers for resources, you should consider personal characteristics, competency levels, and availability of the potential team members. Which of the following processes describes negotiations accurately?

    A. A tool and technique of Staff Acquisition

    B. A tool and technique of Resource Planning

    C. A tool and technique of Organizational Planning

    D. A tool and technique of Team Development

14. You are a project manager working on a new ad campaign for the holiday season. Part of this project entails a series of new TV commercials. You contracted out the production of the commercials that will air during the busy buying season. Now all of the work of the project is done, and you're in the process of closing out the project. You're gathering information from team members and the vendor—including some detailed technical specifications for the commercials that were produced by the vendor—to archive. Which of the following options contains this information, given the circumstances in this question? Choose the best answer.

    A. Administrative documentation

    B. Product documentation

    C. Contract documentation

    D. Other project records

15. You are a project manager for Time Will Tell, an international watch manufacturer. Your project entails developing a watch with global positioning satellite (GPS) capabilities. Kit is a junior staff member with two years of experience in GPS technology. Carrie is a senior staff member with five years of experience working with GPS technology. You are developing the activity duration estimates for the project activities. Carrie is currently working on another project, and it isn't known yet if she'll be available to work on your project. As a result, you've added additional time to Kit's activities, because she isn't as experienced as Carrie and it will likely take her longer to complete them. All of the following statements are true except:

    A. You are considering the resource requirements input of this process.

    B. You're attempting to determine the activity duration estimates output, which includes qualitative assessments of the likely number of work periods.

    C. You are considering the resource capabilities input of this process.

    D. Resource requirements consider the influence resources assigned to each activity have on the duration of the activity.

16. You are scheduled to take the PMP exam next month and are certain you're going to pass. You attended a local college that held a six-week course on passing the PMP, and you've spent a lot of time studying. You've taken two different sample exams and have passed both of those in the 90 percent range. This morning's paper listed a job that you're perfect for. You have all the experience they're looking for and you've met the education requirements. The only piece that's missing is the PMP requirement. You decide to apply for this job, because you're close to becoming a PMP. All of the following are appropriate actions except:
    A. You indicate on the resume and application that you're sitting for the PMP exam next month.
    B. You are so confident you're going to pass that you put the "PMP" designation next to your name on the resume and application.
    C. You say nothing on the resume or application, since you haven't taken the exam yet.
    D. You tell them at the interview that you're taking the exam next month and hope to pass. If you don't pass, you'll continue studying and retake the exam within the next few months.

17. Which of the following is an example of an imposed date constraint, as defined in the Schedule Development process?
    A. The scheduling and assignment of specialized resources to activities required for a deliverable that was promised to key stakeholders on December 22
    B. The scheduling of an outdoor event no later than December 22 in Phoenix to take advantage of the cooler temperatures
    C. The scheduling of a specific deliverable on the date requested by a key stakeholder
    D. The scheduling of specific work that must be completed outside of the work of the project in order to consider a project deliverable complete.

18. Which of the following statements is true regarding project closeout?
    A. This tool and technique of the Cost Control process requires that processes and procedures be developed for closing out a project.
    B. This output of the Cost Control process requires that processes and procedures be developed for closing out a project.
    C. This output of the Administrative Closure process states that certain industries may have specific requirements for closing out a project.
    D. This tool and technique of the Administrative Closure process states that certain industries may have specific requirements for closing out a project.

**19.** You are working on the communications management plan for your project and have considered the timing and need for updated information by your stakeholders. Your organization has modern, up-to-date technology that your stakeholders and staff have used before, so you anticipate that supplying the information and updates to your stakeholders and team members will be a breeze. And, given the short duration of this project, you don't believe the system will require any upgrades during the project. Which of the following does this question describe?

   **A.** Communications requirements

   **B.** Communications technology

   **C.** Communications management plan

   **D.** Information distribution systems

**20.** Your project's primary constraint is time. One of your key stakeholders (who is a major contributor on this project) is demanding the schedule be lengthened. She held her department picnic last weekend, and three of her staff members came down with West Nile virus. The team members she's assigned to your project (who didn't contract the virus) must now do double duty and help support the department functions until their co-workers get well. Your customer will not agree to a schedule change. Which of the following statements is false given the facts in this question?

   **A.** The project manager has the weakest amount of power and authority in this type of organization.

   **B.** The project manager should try to resolve the problem such that it doesn't affect the project schedule.

   **C.** This company's organizational structure is functional, since the department manager is responsible for assigning resources to the project.

   **D.** The project manager should work with the stakeholder to resolve the problem and negotiate with the customer to change the schedule.

**21.** All of the following statements are true regarding quality audits except:

   **A.** The primary purpose of quality audits is to identify lessons learned.

   **B.** Quality audits are a tool and technique of the Quality Control process.

   **C.** Quality audits can be performed at random.

   **D.** Quality audits can be performed on a schedule.

**22.** You are a contract project manager and have entered into the requirements-gathering phase of your project. Two of the departments you're working with on this project have competing interests regarding this project and have done everything they can, including sabotage, to undermine the work so far. In order to finish up the requirements-gathering phase, you will have to exert some influence. Which of the following statements is not true regarding influencing the organization?

  **A.** Influencing entails the ability to get things done.

  **B.** Influencing requires an understanding of the formal and informal structures of the organization, including the use of power and politics.

  **C.** Power involves getting the people in these two departments to do things they wouldn't otherwise do.

  **D.** Power entails getting these two departments with competing interests cooperating effectively to achieve the goals of the project.

**23.** When the individual activities are very accurately detailed, which of the following cost estimating techniques is the best to use and why?

  **A.** Bottom-up estimating, because accurate details at the activity level increase the accuracy of this process, which also increases the cost of this technique.

  **B.** Analogous estimating, because it is less costly than other techniques but is typically the most accurate because you're basing cost information on previous projects and activities that are very similar in fact, not just appearance.

  **C.** Parametric modeling cost and accuracy are very predictable, because they use known project characteristics in a mathematical model to produce costs estimates.

  **D.** Expert judgment, because it is less costly than other techniques but usually the most accurate, because the people estimating the costs have previous experience with other similar activities.

**24.** Which of the following tells you how much more budget is required to finish the project if everything continues at the current levels of performance?

  **A.** AC

  **B.** ETC

  **C.** EAC

  **D.** EV

**25.** Information-gathering techniques used in the Risk Identification process include all of the following except:

  **A.** Brainstorming

  **B.** Delphi technique

  **C.** Interviewing

  **D.** Checklists

**26.** All of the following statements are true regarding motivational theories except for which one?

   **A.** Motivational theories present ideas on why people act the way they do.

   **B.** Motivational theories present ideas on how to influence people to act the way you want to get the results you want.

   **C.** Motivational theories include extrinsic motivators, like religious influences, and intrinsic motivators like self achievement.

   **D.** Maslow and Herzberg are two well-known theorists on the topic of motivation.

**27.** Which of the following describes the interaction between the project management processes endorsed by PMI?

   **A.** The Executing process is the only input to the Closing process.

   **B.** The Planning process inputs are Initiating and Controlling.

   **C.** The Planning process is the only input to the Executing process.

   **D.** The Controlling and Planning processes are both inputs and outputs to each other.

**28.** What is the present value of $8,000 received three years from now using a seven percent interest rate? Assume all options are rounded to the nearest whole dollar.

   **A.** $9,800

   **B.** $6,530

   **C.** $9,680

   **D.** $6,612

**29.** You are a project manager for Rhone Valley Importers. Your buyer has found a new product for a project you're working on that she's convinced will sell well in this country. Taking on this new product introduces a considerable opportunity for the company but at the same time is also a considerable threat. The cost of this product exceeds anything your company has imported before, and if it doesn't sell as well as the buyer thinks it will, the company could go into bankruptcy. You have the authority to sign this vendor on with the organization. You and the buyer are long-time friends and have discussed the possibility of starting your own company many times. You both look at each other and have the same thought at the same time: This product could be the hit product that will launch your new business. Which of the following steps should you take? Choose the best answer.

   **A.** The risk in this venture is significant to the organization, so you should inform the project sponsor and the stakeholders about the threat it could pose and seek their approval before signing on the vendor.

   **B.** You believe this is a good opportunity for the company, even though the risk is high. There are no conflict of interest problems, so you decide to sign on the vendor.

   **C.** The risk in this venture is significant to the organization, but the potential for gain is great. There is no personal gain at stake in this venture, so you decide to sign on the vendor.

   **D.** You turn in your resignation, without saying anything about the new product, and start a new company with your buyer friend and hire the vendor she found.

30. Your project sponsor has reviewed the initial project schedule you created for the project. She is not happy with the project end date, because it doesn't match the promise date she gave the customer. You decide to use some compression techniques first. Which of the following statements should you keep in mind (and know to be true) regarding duration compression?

    A. Crashing is a compression technique that typically produces a viable alternative.

    B. Fast tracking is a compression technique that typically results in increased costs.

    C. Compression shortens the project schedule but doesn't change project scope.

    D. Crashing is a compression technique that typically results in increased risk.

31. You are a project manager working on a new scientific discovery in conjunction with your local university. Due to some changes that were approved during the Controlling process, you discover that the description of the project's product is no longer accurate or complete. Which of the following tools and techniques (associated with the process it occurs in) will you use to correct this problem?

    A. Scope change control system in Scope Change Control

    B. Quality control system in Quality Control

    C. Configuration management in Integrated Change Control

    D. Change control system in Integrated Change Control

32. Which of the following statements is not true regarding Project Management Knowledge Areas?

    A. They are a collection of processes that share similar themes.

    B. They benefit from the specific knowledge and skills centered in each area and bring together processes that have things in common.

    C. There are nine knowledge areas.

    D. They are assigned to specific project life cycle phases and are performed only during that life cycle phase.

33. You have used several cash flow methods to determine alternative ways of performing your current project. You know which of the following is true regarding the results of your cash flow analysis?

    A. Payback period and IRR will generally give you the same accept/reject decision.

    B. NPV and discounted cash flows will generally give you the same accept/reject decision.

    C. Payback period and discounted cash flows will generally give you the same accept/reject decision.

    D. NPV and IRR will generally give you the same accept/reject decision.

**34.** You've just been assigned a new project. You have a copy of the project charter close at hand. It identifies you as the project manager, and after reading it over you believe most of the deliverables are identified. But when reading over the product description you notice a deliverable that wasn't identified in the project charter. Which of the following statements is *not* true based on the information in this question?

   **A.** The product description describes the characteristics of the product of the project, so the new deliverable should be incorporated into the scope statement.

   **B.** The product description includes the product requirements, which represent agreed-upon customer needs.

   **C.** The progressive elaboration of the product description will occur throughout the Planning process and is a tool and technique of the Scope Planning process.

   **D.** The product description includes the product design, which reflects the product requirements.

**35.** You are contracting services for your current project. You need three chemical engineers to work on your project and you'll need specialized equipment and supplies to execute the project. The vendor has agreed to set the rates for the engineers at $275 per hour. The specialized equipment and supplies will be charged back to your organization as they're needed and purchased for the project. What type of contract is this?

   **A.** Fixed price

   **B.** Time and materials

   **C.** Cost-reimbursable

   **D.** Cost-reimbursable plus incentive

**36.** You are a project manager for Jungle Tykes Outdoor Equipment. Your organization supplies playground equipment to several major city parks and schools in the U.S. You are working with the marketing team to design a new piece of equipment. You are in the early stages of project planning and decide that "a small number of prototype testers" is an accurate enough description for the resources needed during the prototyping phase. You're guessing (based on past experience with a similar project) once the prototype is designed and functional, you'll need to bring in a specific number of experts to test it. Which of the following best describes the portion of the Resource Planning process this question refers to?

   **A.** Resource pool description

   **B.** Expert judgment

   **C.** Resource requirements

   **D.** Activity duration estimates

37. Which process is the foundation process within the Risk Management knowledge area that helps establish risk management for all the processes that follow?
    A. Risk Planning
    B. Risk Response Planning
    C. Risk Management Planning
    D. Risk Identification

38. All of these statements describe the Project Scope Management knowledge area except which of the following?
    A. It's concerned with defining all of the work of the project.
    B. It has five processes.
    C. Its processes occur in four of the five project life cycle phases.
    D. It's similar to Project Quality Management in that both knowledge areas are concerned with the product of the project meeting the requirements of the project.

39. If EV = 145, PV = 162, AC = 138, BAC = 200, and ETC = 62, what is EAC when you believe current variances are not typical?
    A. 201
    B. 190.4
    C. 193
    D. 200

40. You are in the midst of performing the Project Cost Management knowledge area. You discover there are two competing alternatives to decide between. You can hire a contractor to build one of the project's deliverables, or you can buy the deliverable from an overseas supplier. Both options require acquisition, operating, and disposal costs that you compare between the two alternatives to make a decision. What is this technique called?
    A. Value Engineering
    B. Life cycle costing
    C. Earned Value Management
    D. Financial analysis

41. According to the Team Development process, individual development of team members (both managerial and technical skill development) is important for all of the following reasons except:
    A. Individual development is the foundation of team building, so without it, teams may not function as well as they could.
    B. Any training needed for individual development should be completed prior to the assignment of the individuals to the team.
    C. Individual development enhances the ability of the team to function as a team.
    D. Team development is critical in achieving the goals and objectives of the project. Therefore, individual development is critical to achieving the goals and objectives of the project.

42. Your project requires three resources with specific knowledge of aeronautics. Fortunately, your organization has these individuals on staff. The project will be influenced as a result of their skills and knowledge, and you know that certain aspects of the project work will have to be organized in a way that will accommodate their special knowledge. Which of the following best describes this concept?

    A. Expected staff assignments

    B. Preferences of the project management team

    C. Technical interfaces

    D. Resource requirements

43. You are a project manager for Katie's Kitchen. They market and sell homemade sauces to gourmet grocery store chains and upscale restaurants. Your project concerns adding two new machines to the production line. You have just finished calculating potential dates for each of your activities. The "Prepare Flooring" activity is scheduled for an early start date of May 16, an early finish date of May 30, a late start date of June 1, and a late finish date of June 15. The float for this activity is zero. The "Install Lighting" activity is scheduled for an early start date of June 3, an early finish date of June 30, a late start date of July 1, and a late finish date of July 28. The float for this activity is two days. All other activities have zero float and total 320 days. Which of the following statements is true? Choose the best answer.

    A. The CP for this project is 335 days taking into account the multiple activity duration estimates provided using expert judgment techniques.

    B. CPM calculates multiple duration estimates.

    C. The CP for this project is 348 days taking into account the multiple activity duration estimates provided using expert judgment techniques.

    D. Using float to determine the activities with the least scheduling flexibility is a function of the CPM method.

44. The Information Distribution process consists of all of the following except which one?

    A. Communication skills, which are used in the exchange of information.

    B. Project presentations, which are ways of presenting project information to stakeholders and others

    C. Project records, which are outputs of this process and include status reports and meeting minutes

    D. Retrieval systems, which are ways of getting the information to the project team members and stakeholders

**45.** You are the director of the project management office (PMO) for your organization. Terri, an employee from another department, has approached you about a new project that is being talked about in her department. Terri would like the opportunity to head up this project and wants to convince you of her knowledge of project management and that she can do this job. Terri's goal statement for the project says the following, "Convert all our distribution centers in the USA to Radio Frequency Identification (RFID) tags. This new technology will improve inventory management by giving us a real-time view of demand for the products we sell. It will also help reduce theft and reduce stock-outs. The electronic identification stored in the tags should be fixed. This new technology will require the installation of readers at each warehouse gate." All of the following statements are correct regarding Terri's goal statement except for which one?

- **A.** This statement describes an overview of the project, but it cannot be considered a goal statement because it's missing some important elements.
- **B.** Requirements are specifications of the goal or deliverable, while goals describe what it is the project is trying to produce or accomplish.
- **C.** This statement describes the goals of the project adequately; however, requirements have been added into the statement. These could be included in a project overview but should not be stated in the goals statement.
- **D.** Requirements have been mixed into the statement Terri wrote. One of the requirements in this statement is, "Electronic identification stored in the tags should be fixed."

**46.** The first input listed in the options below is unique to the Scope Change Control process, and the second input listed in the options below is found in four of the seven Controlling processes.

- **A.** Performance reports, work results
- **B.** WBS, work results
- **C.** Performance reports, change requests
- **D.** WBS, change requests

**47.** You are working on documenting the scope statement for your project. You've interviewed the customer and the key stakeholders. Before publishing the scope statement you ask the key stakeholders to review it. Amy, one of your key stakeholders, tells you that you've missed a project objective. John heard about Amy's comment and tells you that the project objective she identified does not impact the success of the project and doesn't need to be documented in the scope statement. In the interest of time, John would like you to get this scope statement approved and published so that the work of the project can begin. Which of the following statements is *not* true given the facts in this question?

- **A.** The scope statement, like the project charter, documents the objectives and deliverables of the project. Each project has only one project charter and one scope statement.

However, changes to the scope statement are to be expected throughout the Planning process.

- **B.** The scope statement contains the objectives and deliverables of the project and is the basis of an agreement between the project team and project customer regarding these elements.
- **C.** The scope statement becomes the basis for future project decisions and provides everyone involved on the project with a fundamental understanding of the work of the project.
- **D.** The scope statement should identify all project objectives and deliverables, so the missing objective should be added.

**48.** The difference between project deliverables and project requirements is best described in which of the following options?
- **A.** Deliverables are specific items that must be produced to consider the project or project phase complete. Each project phase has only one deliverable, which may have multiple requirements.
- **B.** Requirements are measurable items that must be produced to consider the project or project phase complete. Each project phase may have multiple deliverables with multiple requirements.
- **C.** Requirements are measurable items that must be produced to consider the project or project phase complete; deliverables are the specifications used to tell you what you are trying to produce.
- **D.** Deliverables are specific items that must be produced to consider the project or project phase complete; requirements are the specifications of the deliverables used to tell you if the deliverable was produced successfully.

**49.** You are working on the risk management plan for your current project and need to document how the risk activities will be recorded for the benefit of future projects. Which part of the risk management plan addresses these issues?
- **A.** Lessons learned
- **B.** Thresholds
- **C.** Tracking
- **D.** Reporting format

**50.** Which of the following best describes a project assumption?
- **A.** The equipment needed for the second deliverable of the project will be delivered one week prior to the start of the work for this deliverable
- **B.** The project's allotted budget is $425,000 but you know this is only a rough estimate and will be changed as the project plan is further developed
- **C.** Organizational structure
- **D.** Project schedule

**51.** You are a project manager for Elk Mountain Ink, and your company manufactures ink primarily for the newspaper industry. One of the deliverables of your project entails purchasing new manufacturing equipment that will decrease production times. You've outlined two alternatives based on an initial investment of $76,000. Alternative A has a payback period of 27 months. Alternative B has initial cash inflows of $18,000 semi-annually for the first two years and cash inflows of $4,000 per quarter thereafter. Which alternative should you choose?

   **A.** A decision cannot be made based on this information alone, because the payback periods are the same.

   **B.** Alternative A, because its payback period is shorter than Alternative B's payback period.

   **C.** Alternative B, because its payback period is shorter than Alternative A's payback period.

   **D.** A decision cannot be made, because there is not enough information in the question to determine the best alternative.

**52.** You are working in the Scope Definition process of your project. You have decomposed your deliverables as follows: Project Management, Detailed Planning, Manufacturing, and Testing. The Detailed Planning deliverable is further decomposed to include these deliverables: design document, dimensional restrictions, and user documentation. Adequate cost and duration estimates have now been applied to all the deliverables. Which of the following has occurred in this question?

   **A.** All the steps of decomposition have been performed.

   **B.** Steps one, two, and three of decomposition have been performed for the Detailed Planning deliverable.

   **C.** Only steps one and two of decomposition have been performed for all the deliverables.

   **D.** Step one and step three of decomposition have been performed for all the deliverables with the exception of the Detailed Planning deliverable.

**53.** Your selection committee can only choose one of the following projects: Project A's original investment is $1 million and the payback period is 18 months. Project B's original investment is $1.4 million and the payback period is 18 months. Project C's original investment is $1.8 million and the payback period is 18 months. Which project should the committee choose?

   **A.** Project A

   **B.** Project B

   **C.** Project C

   **D.** There isn't enough information in the question to determine an answer.

54. This tool and technique of the Quality Planning process helps the project team anticipate and identify where quality problems might occur on the project, which in turn, helps them develop alternatives for dealing with the quality problems.

    A. Benefit/cost analysis
    B. Benchmarking
    C. Flowcharting
    D. Design of experiments

55. What are the outputs of the Risk Identification process?

    A. Risks, triggers, and inputs to other processes
    B. Risks, triggers, secondary risks, and inputs to other processes
    C. List of prioritized risks, triggers, and inputs to other processes
    D. List of prioritized risks, residual risks, secondary risks, triggers, and inputs to other processes

56. You are working on a project and are performing the Qualitative Risk Analysis process. You have identified cost, schedule, functionality, and quality risks and assigned each of them a risk ranking of high, medium, or low. Which of the following statements is true? Choose the best answer.

    A. Cost, schedule, functionality, and quality risks can be evaluated separately using their own independent ratings.
    B. Cost, schedule, functionality, and quality risks require both qualitative and quantitative analysis because of their impacts to the project objectives.
    C. Cost, schedule, functionality, and quality risks are risk categories, which are an input to this process.
    D. The risk rankings assigned to cost, schedule, functionality, and quality risk rankings are cardinal values.

57. You have received estimates for one of your project tasks as follows: The pessimistic estimate is 24 days, the optimistic estimate is 18 days, and the most likely estimate is 20 days. What is the standard deviation?

    A. 1
    B. .33
    C. .67
    D. 1.5

58. The correct order of performing the Schedule Development, Cost Budgeting, and Project Plan Development processes is which of the following?
    A. Schedule Development and Project Plan Development can be performed independently, as long as they are both performed before the Cost Budgeting process begins.
    B. Schedule Development must be performed prior to Cost Budgeting, which must be performed before the Project Plan Development process begins.
    C. Cost Budgeting must be performed prior to Schedule Development, which must be performed before the Project Plan Development process begins.
    D. Schedule Development and Cost Budgeting can be performed independently, as long as they are both performed before the Project Plan Development process begins.

59. Which of the following statements explains one of the purposes of the Team Development process? Choose the best answer.
    A. To create an open environment for stakeholders and team members to contribute
    B. To create a disciplined environment for team members to contribute
    C. To create a collocated environment for team members to contribute
    D. To create a collocated, disciplined environment for stakeholders and team members to contribute

60. One of the factors this theory proposes is the importance of friendship and a sense of camaraderie with other team members. Which theory does this describe?
    A. Expectancy Theory
    B. Achievement Theory
    C. Hygiene Theory
    D. Theory X

61. What three types of reports are used in the Performance Reporting process?
    A. Earned value analysis, variance analysis, and trend analysis
    B. Project plan updates, work results, and performance reports
    C. Performance reviews, performance reports, and work results
    D. Status reports, progress reports, and forecasting

62. Performance measurements are a tool and technique of the Schedule Control process. Which of the following measurements pertain to the Schedule Control process?
    A. CPI, EAC
    B. SP, CPI
    C. CP, EAC
    D. SV, SPI

**63.** Your organization is experiencing a shakeup at the top levels of management. Your project team has expressed concerns that their project may be cancelled because of the changes going on at the top. Sure enough, your project team was correct in their suspicions. You've received notice that the project is canceled. Your vendor only has one remaining deliverable for the project scheduled for completion next month. You notify the vendor in writing that the project has been canceled, but you understand there is one more deliverable they need to complete in order to close out the contract. You also notify them that the Phase II portion of the project has been canceled, so current contract negotiations for that portion of the project will end immediately. All of the following processes should be performed given the circumstances in this question except:

   **A.** Lessons Learned

   **B.** Administrative Closure

   **C.** Scope Verification

   **D.** Contract Closeout

**64.** Which of the following statements is *not* true regarding the Scope Definition process?

   **A.** The Scope Definition process is critical for project success.

   **B.** The Scope Definition process improves cost, duration, and resource estimate accuracy.

   **C.** The Scope Definition process allows the project manager to make clear responsibility assignments.

   **D.** The Scope Definition process allows for constituent components to be decomposed to the deliverable level.

# PMP Final Exam Review 3

1. You are a project manager who is managing a large project with multi-national subproject managers under you. Many of your subproject managers are from countries other than your own. You hold a project management meeting and require all the subproject managers to attend. One of the team members from America, who is working in Turkey, seems to be despondent and depressed. You speak with him after the meeting and determine which of the following? Choose the best answer.

   A. He needs some diversity training.
   B. He is perceiving his experiences incorrectly and needs some time off to get his bearings.
   C. He is having trouble maintaining personal integrity.
   D. He is experiencing culture shock.

2. If EV = 145, PV = 162, AC = 138, BAC = 200, and ETC = 62, what is EAC when you expect project performance to continue with the same type of variance that you've experienced to date?

   A. 201
   B. 190.4
   C. 200
   D. 193

3. What plan from a prior process is put into action during the Information Distribution Process? Choose the best answer.

   A. Scope management plan
   B. Resource management plan
   C. Project plan
   D. Communications management plan

4. You are a project manager for Lightening Bolt Enterprises. Your new project involves the research and development of a new type of rechargeable battery. You are still elaborating the product characteristics. One of your stakeholders requests a change. They've filled out a change request form indicating that the change affects the product scope and is essential for a successful project. Which of the following statements is *not* true with regard to the product characteristics?

   A. Product characteristics will be progressively elaborated throughout several project phases and will contain more detail in the later phases.
   B. The change is identified as a product scope change and is classified as essential. Both of these elements—identification and classification—are defined during the Scope Definition process.
   C. Since the product characteristics are still being elaborated, an identification and classification system is absolutely essential.
   D. The product description, even though it's still being progressively elaborated, is an input to the Scope Planning process.

5. You are the project manager for a construction project. Your company is expanding a highway on the east side of town, including revamping the bridges and constructing new on-ramps and off-ramps. Because of the timelines for this project and the heavy traffic at rush hour, you have several teams of resources who will be working around the clock (according to their assigned schedule). The calendar used to construct the project schedule must take the 24-hour workday into account. One group of resources—the asphalt crew—can only work during the first and second shifts. Which of the following statements is true regarding this question? Choose the best answer.

   A. The project calendar, an input to the Schedule Development process, should reflect the asphalt crew's availability.

   B. The resource calendar, a tool and technique of the Schedule Development process, should reflect the asphalt crew's availability.

   C. The resource calendar, an input to the Schedule Development process, should reflect the asphalt crew's availability.

   D. The project calendar, a tool and technique of the Schedule Development process, should reflect the asphalt crew's availability.

6. You've gathered cost estimates for the activities of your current project. Most of the activities can be completed with existing staff resources. The summary cost estimate for existing resources is $535,000. You will also need to hire contractors to perform some of the activities that require specialized skills. You've received a bid from a local vendor for $137,000 for these services. All of the following statements are true except:

   A. You've determined a quantitative estimate of the cost to the organization to perform the activities of the project.

   B. The cost of the vendor services to your organization is considered pricing (from the vendor's perspective), which is a business decision on their part.

   C. When a project is performed under contract, quantitative cost estimates determine how much the organization will charge for producing the product or service of the project.

   D. Your next step should be to develop the cost management plan, which will describe how variances in cost will be managed.

7. You're in the midst of managing a project for the water and sanitation district of your local city. It's a large, complicated project that you've divided into smaller, manageable subprojects, each with their own project managers who all report to you. You know that specific technical elements must be adhered to in the design and implementation of this project due to regulations governing the water and sanitation district. One of the subproject managers (whom you know very well) is a PMP but has never heard of the *PMP Code of Professional Conduct*. What should you do?

   A. You know this person very well and know they have a high level of integrity. It isn't necessary for them to read the *PMP Code of Professional Conduct*.

   B. Tell them where to find a copy of the *PMP Code of Professional Conduct* on the PMI website (or give them a copy) and require them to read it.

   C. Put a copy of the *PMP Code of Professional Conduct* on their desk when they're not looking and assume they'll read it.

   D. Let them have your copy of the *PMP Code of Professional Conduct* and suggest they read it.

8. The purpose of this process is to determine what consequences the identified risks will have on the project objectives and the probability that they'll occur. This process puts risks in priority order according to their effect on the project objectives and assigns an overall risk ranking for the project. What process does this describe?

    A. Risk Identification
    B. Qualitative Risk Analysis
    C. Risk Management Planning
    D. Quantitative Risk Analysis

9. You are working on a project in the automotive industry that requires specialized knowledge of robotics. You know that one full-time expert with skills in this area will be needed during the design phase and again in the deployment phase of this project. During design this expert will work on several activities that were decomposed from the deliverable called "Mechanical Design," and during deployment they will work on the activities decomposed from the deliverable called "Install Arm." You derived this information from both the scope statement and the WBS. You've received some initial estimates of approximately $225 an hour for this resource. Which of the following best describes the process or processes used to derive the information in this question?

    A. The scope statement and the WBS are inputs to both the Resource Planning process and the Cost Estimating process.
    B. The scope statement and the WBS are inputs to the Activity Definition process.
    C. The scope statement and the WBS are inputs to both Activity Definition process and the Cost Estimating process.
    D. The scope statement and the WBS are inputs to the Resource Planning process.

10. Which of the following are the most essential general management skills needed during the Project Plan Execution process?

    A. Leadership, communication, and negotiation
    B. Communication, general business knowledge, and budgeting skills
    C. Communication, negotiation, and problem solving skills
    D. Leadership, communication, and general business knowledge skills

11. What is the future value of $10,000 two years from now using a five percent interest rate? Assume all options are rounded to the nearest whole dollar.

    A. $10,025
    B. $9,070
    C. $9,090
    D. $11,025

12. As a result of performing this process, change requests may occur.
    A. Quality Assurance
    B. Cost Control
    C. Project Plan Execution
    D. Integrated Change Control

13. You are in the Scope Planning process. You're using techniques such as value engineering, value analysis, function analysis, and quality function deployment. What tool and technique of this process are you using?
    A. Benefit/cost analysis
    B. Product analysis
    C. Earned value analysis
    D. Benchmarking

14. Your project sponsor has asked you to monitor the project management process. What tool and technique of the Quality Control process will you use?
    A. Control charts
    B. Pareto diagrams
    C. Flowcharting
    D. Trend analysis

15. Your company manufactures a line of automotive cleaning products. Your assignment entails designing a new line of soap for car washes. You've decided to go straight to the customer to define what qualities and needs they desire regarding the new product. You start by holding a series of focus group meetings to find out the basic needs. Next, you develop a sample car wash soap that you give to a selected group of potential customers to try out. They give you great feedback and suggestions that you use to further develop the product. Which of the following describes this process?
    A. Phase sequencing
    B. Leveling
    C. Fast tracking
    D. Progressive elaboration

16. What are the tools and techniques of the Organizational Planning process?
    A. Organizational theory, alternatives identifications, stakeholder analysis, and templates
    B. Human resource practices, organizational theory, and alternatives identifications
    C. Organizational theory, stakeholder analysis, and expert judgment
    D. Templates, human resource practices, organizational theory, and stakeholder analysis.

17. The effectiveness of this process will determine whether risk increases or decreases for the project.
    A. Risk Monitoring and Control
    B. Risk Response Planning
    C. Risk Management Planning
    D. Risk Identification

18. You are wrapping up the Closing processes for your project. You've notified the seller that the terms of the contract have been satisfied, and you've created a set of indexed records. All of the following statements are true regarding this question except which one? Choose the least correct answer.
    A. The indexed records become inputs to the Administrative Closure process, which are known as other project records.
    B. Contract Closure is performed before the Administrative Closure process.
    C. This question is referring to the output called contract file.
    D. Indexed records are the project records created during the Administrative Closure process.

19. You work for a specialized book publisher that publishes 35 new titles per year. Your company has a specific process in place for managing each phase of a book's release. One of their requirements is the design phase must be approved by an associate publisher before it is handed off to the production phase. You're accepting your first assignment as the project manager for a new publication. You're responsible for seeing this project through from the beginning (assigning a qualified author to write on this topic) to the end (distributing the book to wholesalers and retailers). What does this scenario describe?
    A. Organizational Planning
    B. Phase sequencing
    C. Fast tracking
    D. Scope verification

20. The Quality Control process is concerned with all of the following except which one? Choose the least correct answer.
    A. Product results
    B. Cost and schedule performance
    C. Rebaselining
    D. Eliminating unsatisfactory results

21. Your customer has decided that you cannot go forward with the project you're managing without a change to the agreed-upon WBS. A contract amendment is agreed upon and signed, the change control system processes are followed, and you modify the appropriate planning documents to reflect the change. As a result of the approved change, substantial changes to the project costs and the project schedule occur as well. What must occur next and why? Choose the best answer.

    A. Baselines must be adjusted to reflect the new project costs and schedule.

    B. Corrective actions are taken, which in turn generate change requests that are managed through the scope change control system.

    C. Updates to the scope management plan are made to reflect the approved project change.

    D. Lessons learned are documented so that future projects take into consideration the impact of the change to this WBS.

22. Which of the following statements regarding cash flow analysis techniques is *not* true?

    A. The discounted cash flow technique differs from NPV in that the discounted cash flow technique compares cash inflows as a total, while NPV calculates cash inflows period by period and then totals the PV of each period.

    B. The discounted cash flow technique and the NPV technique both take the time value of money into consideration.

    C. NPV is the most conservative cash flow analysis technique and assumes reinvestment at the cost of capital.

    D. The discounted cash flow technique may use future value and present value formulas to determine the value of the investment or return. It's the least precise of all the cash flow calculations.

23. You are evaluating vendor proposals and using selection criteria in order to choose a vendor. One of the criteria states that resources are required to have civil engineering degrees and a minimum of three years of experience. Which of the following tools and techniques does this question refer to?

    A. Weighting systems
    B. Contract negotiation
    C. Independent estimate
    D. Screening systems

24. The expected cost of the work when completed is which of the following?

    A. AC
    B. EV
    C. ETC
    D. EAC

25. You've applied for and accepted a new position advertised as a project manager. Things unfortunately don't go well from that point on. Within two weeks of starting the job, Jim, who is one of your project team members, enters a dispute with you over the work you've assigned him. You haven't been able to successfully resolve the dispute with Jim, and you are determined to get to the bottom of things quickly. You call a meeting with Jim's manager, who is your peer. She subsequently informs you that everything Jim has told you about his availability and task assignments are true. Together, you and Jim's manager work out a reasonable solution to the problem. What type of organization does this describe?

    A. Weak matrix

    B. Strong matrix

    C. Functional

    D. Balanced matrix

26. You are working on a top-secret project for a medical research firm. The project sponsor won't admit in public to being the project sponsor for your project. Most of the project team members do not know who the other team members are. Due to the nature of this project and the high secrecy level, you've determined that some of the activities of the project may be performed only in part. Which mathematical analysis technique does this question describe? Choose the best answer.

    A. CPM

    B. GERT

    C. PERT

    D. EVM

27. The project manager's role as it relates to the project charter includes all of the following except which one?

    A. The project manager assumes responsibility for the success of the project starting after the publication of the project charter.

    B. The project charter identifies the project manager who will use the charter as a guideline to develop the project plan.

    C. The project manager's primary responsibilities include initiating, planning, and executing the project according to the project charter.

    D. The project manager will use the project charter to help identify activities, tasks, resources requirements, project costs, and more during the Planning phase of the project.

28. Project management processes must be applied to the Contract Administration process in order to manage contractual relationships and to integrate the outputs of which of the following processes?

    A. Project Plan Execution, Performance Reporting, Quality Control, and Change Control
    B. Project Plan Execution, Quality Assurance, Change Control, and Scope Verification
    C. Performance Reporting, Quality Control, Scope Verification, and Change Control
    D. Project Plan Execution, Performance Reporting, Quality Assurance, and Scope Verification

29. You are very interested in becoming a project manager. You have mentored with other experienced project managers in your organization to learn more about how to be an effective project manager. You've been told your organizational skills and communication skills are excellent. However, you need some additional training in accounting and budgeting skills, as you are weak in these general management areas. The mentor who was honest enough to tell you this explained it which of the following ways?

    A. You will not be able to sit for the PMP exam unless get formal training in the general management areas.
    B. General management skills are very likely to affect project outcomes. If you lack any of these skills, it could affect your project and your career adversely, so you should get some training in these areas.
    C. The Cost Budgeting and Cost Control processes are under the Planning Processes group, and you will not be able to pass the questions on the PMP exam that pertain to these processes if you don't get some training.
    D. General management skills are important to your project outcomes, and Cost Budgeting and Cost Control are two of the most important processes within the Executing phase of a project, so you should get some training in these areas.

30. You are in the process of attaining and hiring resources for the project. Some of the resources can be found from within the organization, but three of the resources you've identified must be hired on contract. Your organization has strict policies regarding staff assignments, and you must make certain there is no one in your organization with the same skills of the contractors you're considering hiring. Which of the following best describes the input this question outlines?

    A. Staffing requirements
    B. Project staff
    C. Resource pool description
    D. Recruitment practices

**31.** You are the project manager for Changing Tides video games. You have produced a project network diagram and have updated the activity list. Which process have you just finished?

  A. The Activity Sequencing process, which identifies all the specific activities of the project

  B. The Activity Sequencing process, which identifies all the activity dependencies

  C. The Activity Duration Estimating process, which diagrams project network time estimates

  D. The Activity Duration Estimating process, which identifies all the dependent activities of the project

**32.** What are the outputs of the Scope Planning process?

  A. Product analysis, scope statement, and scope management plan

  B. Scope statement, scope management plan, and WBS

  C. Scope statement, supporting detail, and WBS

  D. Scope statement, supporting detail, and scope management plan

**33.** You have proposed a new, high-risk project for your company that will significantly expand its production capabilities. Your company has undertaken other high-risk projects in the past, but never a project like this. However, you're not surprised when you're told your project is approved. Which of the following statements is *not* true?

  A. Organizational cultures have a direct influence on the project.

  B. Your organization is in a leading-edge position within their industry.

  C. Entrepreneurial organizations are likely averse to taking on risky projects.

  D. Your organization has an aggressive culture. Project managers feel free to propose new ideas and projects in this culture.

**34.** Your project requires the procurement of four services from a vendor external to the organization. The remaining services will be procured from within the organization. All of the following statements are true except for which one? Choose the least correct answer.

  A. The processes from Solicitation Planning through Contract Closeout should be performed once for each service being contracted.

  B. All of the processes in the Project Procurement Management knowledge area should be performed at least once for the services being contracted.

  C. Only two processes from the Project Procurement Management knowledge area should be performed for the services you're obtaining from within the organization.

  D. Procurement Planning is performed prior to all other processes in the Project Procurement Management knowledge area.

35. What are the Communication Planning inputs?
    A. Communications requirements, communications technology, and stakeholder analysis
    B. Communications requirements, stakeholder analysis, and constraints
    C. Communications requirements, communications technology, assumptions, and constraints
    D. Communications requirements, constraints, and staffing management plan

36. You are a project manager for an advertising firm. Your project is well underway, and the project plan is being executed. Your customer has requested some changes to the project. These changes will require changes to the project plan, and maybe even changes to the work that's already occurred. This is a highly interactive knowledge area, so you're not surprised that you'll have to repeat the processes. What knowledge area does this question describe?
    A. Project Scope Management
    B. Project Time Management
    C. Project Integration Management
    D. Project Communications Management

37. Your project selection committee is considering four projects. Project A's NPV is positive, it has an IRR of 14 percent, and the payback period is 21 months. Project B's NPV is negative, it has an IRR of 9 percent, and the payback period is 16 months. Project C's NPV is positive, it has an IRR of 16 percent, and the payback period is 18 months. Project D's NPV is negative, it has an IRR of 16 percent, and the payback period is 13 months. Which project should you choose?
    A. Project A
    B. Project B
    C. Project C
    D. Project D

38. Technical risks, organizational risks, and external risks are examples of which of the following?
    A. Risk categories, which are an input to the Risk Identification process
    B. Risk categories, which are a tool and technique of the Risk Identification process
    C. Identified risks, which are an input to the Qualitative Risk Analysis process
    D. Identified risks, which are an input to the Qualitative and Quantitative Risk Analysis process

39. Simulation techniques can be very useful when determining project duration. Which of the following statements describes the most commonly used simulation technique in the Schedule Development process? Choose the best answer.

    A. Earned value analysis. This technique uses a range of probable activity durations for each activity that are then used to calculate a range of probable duration results for the project itself.

    B. Monte Carlo analysis. This technique uses a range of probable activity durations for each activity that are then used to calculate a range of probable duration results for the project itself.

    C. What-if analysis. This technique determines alternative project durations by simulating different situations such as a pending strike or the delay of a major deliverable.

    D. Project management software. This technique allows for what-if analysis and other simulation techniques to determine alternative project durations based on different situations such as a pending strike or the delay of a major deliverable.

40. You've taken over a project that's currently in trouble. You've held a meeting with the key stakeholders to demonstrate the new product prototype. They came prepared with the product requirements and upon inspection inform you that this prototype is not what the customer specified. Your boss instructs you to get the prototype corrected and make it match the requirements the customer specified before holding a demo with the customer. She also warns you to take a look at the work of the project. She's concerned that things aren't happening as planned and that the last project manager was not paying close enough attention to the project plan. Corrections might be needed. What knowledge area does this describe?

    A. Project Time Management

    B. Project Scope Management

    C. Project Integration Management

    D. Project Risk Management

41. You are the project manager for a large project. The projected schedule shows the project is not scheduled for completion for another three years. Some of the stakeholders have changed over the course of this project, and new stakeholders will become involved toward the end of the project. The project team members have also changed as the project has moved on to a new set of deliverables. You are having a difficult time motivating the new team members. The techniques you used with the previous team don't seem to be working with this team. More resources will be brought on and off the project team at various stages throughout the life cycle, so you'd like to resolve this problem soon. You know from studying the Project Human Resource Management knowledge area that you should do which of the following?

    A. The processes in this knowledge area ensure that the human and material resources involved on the project are used in the most effective way possible.

    B. The same communication style should be used throughout the life of the project.

    C. You will change the techniques used to motivate, lead, and coach the human resources involved on the project as the project progresses through the life cycle.

    D. This knowledge area's processes include Organizational Planning, Staff Acquisition, and Team Development.

**42.** Your company, Kick That Ball Sports, has appointed you project manager for their new Cricket product line introduction. This is a national effort, and all the retail stores across the country need to have the new products on the shelves before the media advertising blitz begins. The product line involves three new products, some with multiple deliverables. The Scope Definition process is now complete. Which of the following is true?

   **A.** The WBS template, an output of the Scope Definition process, was used from the previous project to create the WBS for this project. The WBS encompasses the major deliverables for the project.

   **B.** The WBS template from the previous project, an output from the Scope Planning process, was used to create the WBS for this project. The WBS encompasses the major deliverables for the project.

   **C.** The WBS, an output of the Scope Planning process, has been created, and it encompasses the full scope of work for the project.

   **D.** The WBS, an output of the Scope Definition process, has been created, and it encompasses the full scope of work for the project.

**43.** Your selection committee can only choose one of the following projects: Project A's original investment is $1 million, the present value of the cash inflows is $1 million, and the discount rate is eight percent. Project B's original investment is $1.4 million, the present value of the cash inflows is $1.4 million, and the discount rate is seven percent. Project C's original investment is $1.8 million, the present value of the cash inflows is $1.8 million, and the discount rate is six percent. Which project should the committee choose?

   **A.** Project C

   **B.** Project B

   **C.** Project A

   **D.** There isn't enough information in the question to determine an answer.

**44.** You work for Writer's Block, a service that reviews and critiques manuscripts for aspiring writers. You were assigned to be the project manager for a brand-new computer system that logs, tracks, and electronically scans and files all submitted manuscripts along with the editor's notes. You hired and worked with a vendor who wrote the system to your specifications. You are in the Closing processes, and you're reviewing a report regarding certain aspects of the project's performance. The report states the following, "The reviewers recommend that future projects of this nature use a written formal acceptance and closure process. The vendor was notified verbally that the contract was completed when a written process should have been used." Which of the following options contains this information, given the circumstances in this question? Choose the best answer.

   **A.** Lessons learned

   **B.** Performance measurements documentation

   **C.** Procurement audit

   **D.** None of the answers given are correct.

**45.** You are a project manager for the information technology division of a local satellite TV broadcasting company. This spring, the chief information officer for your company gave you the project to convert and upgrade all the PCs in the department to the latest release of a specific desktop application. Prior to this conversion, all manner of desktop software existed on machines throughout the company and had caused increasing problems with sharing files and information across the company. A lot of unproductive hours were spent converting information into several formats. This project came about as a result of which of the following?

   **A.** Business need

   **B.** Market demand

   **C.** Technological advance

   **D.** Social need

**46.** What is the difference between Qualitative Risk Analysis and Quantitative Risk Analysis?

   **A.** Qualitative Risk Analysis uses sensitivity analysis and decision tree analysis as some of its tools and techniques to assess risks and their impacts.

   **B.** Quantitative Risk Analysis uses scales of probability and impact as inputs to the PI matrix. Qualitative Risk Analysis determines interactions among the risks.

   **C.** Quantitative Risk Analysis uses a probability/impact risk rating matrix and risk probability and impact as some of its tools and techniques to assess risks and their impacts.

   **D.** Qualitative Risk Analysis determines the impact and probability of risk events on the project objectives. Quantitative Risk Analysis assigns numeric probabilities to each risk and their impacts on project objectives.

**47.** You are a project manager in Information Technology. Your project involves writing a new software program for the sales team of your company. Your company has strict policies regarding hardware. The project team requested new hardware for this project that was outside the stated policy. The request was denied. As a result, your new program must be compatible on the hardware specified in the policy. This is an example of which of the following?

   **A.** Risk

   **B.** Constraint

   **C.** Deliverable

   **D.** Assumption

**48.** Your project entails building a new customer service call center for an insurance company. The company's strategic plan states that hold times must be reduced by a total of 15 percent over the next two years. In order to accomplish this goal, the new service center must meet exact specifications regarding the placement of cubicles, equipment, and access to customer records. The subproject manager assigned to the equipment deliverable worked on the previous customer service call center that was built on the East Coast. You are certain he is up to speed on the newest equipment updates and needs and will be assigned to your project. This is an example of which of the following?

   **A.** Risk

   **B.** Constraint

   **C.** Requirement

   **D.** Assumption

**49.** All but one of the following statements are true regarding the six needs or demands that typically generate new project work. Which of these statements is *not* true?

   **A.** An example of a business need is an organization authorizing a project to build a new customer service center as a result of an increase in sales.

   **B.** The relationship between the product or service of the project and the need or demand that generated the project should be documented.

   **C.** C. The six needs are market demand, business need, legal requirement, customer request, technological advance, and social need.

   **D.** The six needs represent opportunities, business requirements, or problems to the organization and generally require that management make decisions and respond to the needs or demands.

**50.** You are a project manager for a motivational consulting firm. Your project entails putting together a series of conferences across the country starting 12 months from now. You are diagramming your project, but you've found you must use dummy activities in order to connect all the logical relationships correctly. What diagramming method are you using?

   **A.** PDM

   **B.** Conditional

   **C.** AON

   **D.** ADM

**51.** What are the Quality Planning process outputs?

   **A.** Quality management plan, benchmarking, checklists, and evaluation criteria

   **B.** Quality management plan, benchmarking, and operational definitions

   **C.** Quality management plan, checklists, and inputs to other processes

   **D.** Quality management plan, operational definitions, checklists, and inputs to other processes

52. You are using information-gathering techniques to identify project risks. It's very important that you keep biases to a minimum. Which technique should you use? Choose the best answer.

    A. Interviewing
    B. Delphi
    C. Brainstorming
    D. Nominal group

53. You've developed a risk impact scale as follows: 0.1, 0.3, 0.5, 0.7. Which of the following statements is true regarding this scale?

    A. This is a non-linear cardinal scale that reflects the probability of the risk consequences to the project objectives.
    B. This is a linear cardinal scale that reflects the severity of the effects of the risk consequences to the project objectives.
    C. This is a linear cardinal scale that reflects the probability of the effects of the risk consequences to the project objectives.
    D. This is a linear ordinal scale that reflects the severity of the effects of the risk consequences to the project objectives.

54. You have received estimates for one of your project tasks as follows: The pessimistic estimate is 22 days, the optimistic estimate is 18 days, and the most likely estimate is 20 days. Which of the following options states the expected value and the CPM estimate respectively?

    A. Expected value is 19, and the CPM estimate is 18.
    B. Expected value is 20, and the CPM estimate is 20.
    C. Expected value is 19, and the CPM estimate is 18.
    D. Expected value is 21, and the CPM estimate is 22.

55. Which of the following statements describes the difference between the project plan and the project performance measurement baselines?

    A. The project plan changes as the project progresses and more information is known. Performance measurement baselines typically only changes when the project scope or project deliverables change.
    B. Neither the project plan nor the performance measurement baselines should ever change.
    C. The project plan changes as the project progresses and more information is known. Performance measurement baselines should never change.
    D. The project plan typically only changes when the project scope or project deliverables change. Performance measurement baselines change as the project scope or project deliverables change and those changes are approved.

**56.** The following exchange took place at your last team meeting: "I don't agree with Violet, and I'm not going to stop working on the secret formula just because she doesn't have the equipment in place for the experiments." What stage is this team in?

   **A.** Confrontation

   **B.** Norming

   **C.** Storming

   **D.** Withdrawal

**57.** Your manager storms into your office demanding to know what paragraph three of the recent status report means, even though she clearly knows what it means by the tone in her voice. She wants you to know that, after all, she is the Director of Marketing and has the authority to "do what it takes" to keep you in line. She doesn't appreciate your mention of the items in paragraph three and tells you if you do it again, she'll take further action to make sure you're demoted. Which theory does your manager practice? Choose the best answer.

   **A.** Achievement Theory

   **B.** Expectancy Theory

   **C.** Contingency Theory

   **D.** Theory X

**58.** This tool and technique of the Performance Reporting process is the most commonly used method to measure project performance.

   **A.** Performance reviews

   **B.** Variance analysis

   **C.** Trend analysis

   **D.** Earned value analysis

**59.** You are a project manager with a wide range of experience. You've worked in many different organizations and have seen all of the following terms used for change control board except:

   **A.** TAB

   **B.** TRB

   **C.** ERB

   **D.** CMB

**60.** Which of the following statements is *not* true regarding the identification and classification of scope changes?

   **A.** The process for identifying and classifying scope changes is documented in the scope management plan.

   **B.** Identification and classification is essential when elaborating the product description.

   **C.** Identification and classification is difficult to do when the product description is still being elaborated.

   **D.** Identification and classification involves techniques such as change requests and product skills and knowledge.

**61.** Your CCB has approved a schedule change. You update the schedule and discover that the project end date is significantly different than the original schedule due to the changes in the start and finish dates to some of the critical path activities. What type of schedule update did you make, and what should you consider doing because of the significant change in dates?

   **A.** Revisions, rework

   **B.** Adjusted baseline, schedule updates

   **C.** Revisions, rebaselining

   **D.** Adjusted baseline, corrective action

**62.** Your organization is experiencing a shakeup at the top levels of management. Your project team has expressed concerns that their project may be cancelled because of the changes going on at the top. Sure enough, your project team was correct in their suspicions. You've received notice that the project is canceled. Your vendor only has one remaining deliverable for the project scheduled for completion next month. You notify the vendor in writing that the project has been canceled, but you understand there is one more deliverable they need to complete in order to close out the contract. You also notify them that the Phase II portion of the project has been canceled, so current contract negotiations for that portion of the project will end immediately. Which of the following processes documents the details concerning the amount of work completed at the cancellation date?

   **A.** Lessons Learned

   **B.** Administrative Closure

   **C.** Scope Verification

   **D.** Contract Closeout

**63.** You've recently begun to suspect your friend, a fellow PMP, may be accepting gifts from hardware vendors who are bidding on an upcoming multi-million dollar project that's she's going to manage. She has a new LCD flat-screen computer monitor at her desk, she showed off her new handheld PDA at a meeting two days ago, and today she unpacked a new laptop while you were in her office. Which of the following should you do?

   **A.** You tell your friend these gifts probably aren't appropriate and leave it at that.

   **B.** You and your friend have a long conversation about the items she's received, and she decides to return them and not accept any more items from vendors in the future.

   **C.** You tell your friend you're concerned about the appearance of impropriety because of all the new things she's purchased lately, so you ask her directly if these items were gifts from the vendor or if she purchased them herself.

   **D.** You know this is a conflict of interest situation, and it violates the *PMP Code of Professional Conduct*. You report your friend, so that an investigation can take place.

**64.** You've just been assigned a new project. You have a copy of the project charter close at hand. It identifies you as the project manager, and after reading it over you believe that most of the deliverables are identified. But when reading over the product description you notice a deliverable that wasn't identified in the project charter. You believe this deliverable is a requirement in order to successfully complete this project. You decide to speak with two of the project's key stakeholders to clear this up. Each one of them gives you an alternative way of approaching the project to incorporate the deliverable you discovered in the product description. Which of the following statements is true based on the information in this question?

   **A.** You are working on the scope statement, which is an output of the Scope Planning process. One input to this process and two tools and techniques were described in this question.

   **B.** You are working on updates to the scope statement, which is an output of the Scope Definition process. You should update the scope statement to incorporate the new deliverable and notify all the stakeholders of the modification.

   **C.** You are working on the scope statement, which is an output of the Scope Planning process. Two inputs to this process and two tools and techniques were described in this question.

   **D.** You are working on updates to the scope statement, which is an output of the Scope Definition process. One of the tools and techniques you might consider using from this process to determine which stakeholder's alternative is the best choice is benefit/cost analysis.

# PMP Final Exam Review 4

1. You work in the marketing department of your organization. Your project entails designing and preparing a vendor booth for an upcoming conference. Participating in conferences is something your organization does several times a year. You've just been informed that this conference has been canceled due to lack of interest. Which of the following is true?

   A. Since the conference was canceled and the project cannot be completed, there is no need to perform the Closing processes.

   B. Since conferences are held several times a year, preparing the vendor booth is considered an ongoing operation and doesn't meet definition of a project in *A Guide to the PMBOK*.

   C. Since conferences are held several times a year, preparations for each conference are unique, so this project does meet the definition of a project.

   D. Since the conference was canceled, the goals and objectives of the project couldn't be met. Therefore, only the Project Integration Management processes were completed.

2. You are a project manager working on an important project for your organization. It has high visibility with all the corporate big-wigs and will likely get you a promotion if things go well. So far, the project is ahead of schedule, on budget, and the project plan seems to be occurring as predicted. You're holding an important stakeholder meeting this afternoon that involves five of your top team members. One of your team members shows up to work this morning wearing an objectionable piece of jewelry. The article hanging on the chain is a replica of a part of the human anatomy. Other team members have complained to you that they find the necklace offensive. What action should you take? Choose the best answer.

   A. Say nothing. Your team members are free to wear what they like.

   B. Ask the team member to take off the necklace for the meeting.

   C. Tell the team member to take off the necklace and instruct them not to wear it to work again.

   D. Say nothing. You know this team member very well and are certain they won't wear the necklace to the meeting.

3. You have a team member who is getting out of line at status meetings. You meet with this individual privately to raise your concerns. Your team member tells you what's really on their mind and that they disagree with the way you're executing the activities of a particular deliverable. You let the team member know you understand their concerns but that nonetheless, the work will continue as you've directed and they'll have to accept it. What type of power does this describe?

   A. Referent

   B. Social

   C. Legitimate

   D. Punishment

4. All of the following statements are true regarding risks except for which one? Choose the least correct answer.
   A. Risks might be threats to the objectives of the project.
   B. Risks are certain events that may be threats or opportunities to the objectives of the project.
   C. Risks might be opportunities to the objectives of the project.
   D. Risks have causes and consequences.

5. You are working on a project in the automotive industry that requires specialized knowledge of robotics. You know that one full-time expert with skills in this area will be needed during the design phase and again in the deployment phase of this project. You've received some initial estimates of approximately $225 an hour for this resource. Which of the following best describes the processes involved in this question and why?
   A. Activity Definition and Activity Estimating, because Activity Definition determines what activities will be performed on the project, while Activity Estimating determines the length of time the resource is needed and the cost. Activity Estimating can't occur until Activity Definition is completed. These processes are closely linked.
   B. Resource Planning and Cost Estimating, because Resource Planning determines the physical resources needed for the project (in this case, the robotics expert), while Cost Estimating estimates the costs of the resources needed to complete the activities. These processes are closely linked.
   C. Activity Sequencing and Cost Estimating, because the question states that the expert is needed during two phases of the project (that's Activity Sequencing) and provides the cost of the resource (that's Cost Estimating).
   D. Activity Sequencing and Resource Planning, because the activities have a specific sequence in which resources must be applied (first the design phase, then the deployment phase), and the resources have been identified and estimated.

6. Which of the following statements is *not* true regarding the scope management plan?
   A. The scope management plan should describe how changes to cost, schedule, and quality will be managed.
   B. The scope management plan is a subsidiary component of the project plan.
   C. The scope management plan should describe how scope changes will be identified and classified.
   D. The scope management plan should describe how likely scope change is to occur.

7. All of the following statements are true regarding trend analysis except:
   A. Trend analysis is a tool and technique of the Quality Control process.
   B. Trend analysis is a mathematical formula used to forecast future outcomes.
   C. Trend analysis is a tool and technique of the Performance Reporting process.
   D. Trend analysis is used to analyze how problems occur.

8. Which of the following statements regarding the project champion is *not* true?
   A. The project champion is typically someone well-versed in the technical areas of the project or who has strong industry knowledge regarding the project.
   B. The project champion is often called on to make technical decisions and typically has final authority over project issues concerning technical expertise or industry knowledge.
   C. The project champion can lend credibility to the viability of the project due to their technical expertise.
   D. The project champion is a strong project supporter who tends to focus attention on the project from a technical perspective.

9. You work in a matrix organization. Early on in the project, it was determined that the functional manager who heads up the accounting department will be in charge of the project budget. The project sponsor approaches you with a small bonus check for your excellent work at keeping costs in line with the budget. You think the amount of the bonus check is fair and deserved. All of the following statements are true except for which of the following? Choose the least correct answer.
   A. The reward is appropriately linked to the performance.
   B. Rewards and recognition systems should endorse and reinforce behaviors that are desired.
   C. Rewards and recognition systems are a tool and technique of the Team Development process.
   D. The reward is in line with the performance, and you should accept it.

10. You are a project manager in a construction company. Your project sponsor is an experienced project manager herself. She's worried this project may fall behind schedule, since winter is approaching faster than normal for this time of year. She tells you to begin the building phase, even though the design phase isn't yet completed. Which of the following statements is *not* true?
    A. Time is a constraint.
    B. You're using a fast tracking technique.
    C. Phase sequencing is being ignored.
    D. The project schedule is being compressed.

11. You are the project manager for a construction project. Your company is expanding a highway on the east side of town, including revamping the bridges and constructing new on-ramps and off-ramps. Because of the timelines for this project and the heavy traffic at rush hour, you have several teams of resources who will be working around the clock (according to their assigned schedule). The calendar used to construct the project schedule must take the 24-hour workday into account. Which of the following statements is true regarding this question? Choose the best answer.

    A. The project calendar, an input to the Schedule Development process, should reflect the 24-hour work period.

    B. The resource calendar, a tool and technique of the Schedule Development process, should reflect the 24-hour work period.

    C. The resource calendar, an input to the Schedule Development process, should reflect the 24-hour work period.

    D. The project calendar, a tool and technique of the Schedule Development process, should reflect the 24-hour work period.

12. One of the key project stakeholders on your project is asking for the documentation that records, analyzes, and details the project accomplishments before they'll sign off on final acceptance. Which of the following inputs does this describe?

    A. Procurement audit results, an input to the Contract Closeout process

    B. Other project records, an input to the Administrative Closure process

    C. Project reports, an input to the Contract Closeout process

    D. Performance measurement documentation, an input to the Administrative Closure process

13. Your co-worker, Mishi, is a project manager who has come by this title through experience. He hasn't had any formal training in project management and isn't familiar with PMI techniques. You discover after talking with him that he's afraid to approach a team member with a corrective action, because Mishi doesn't understand general accounting principles. The team member needs to take this action soon, but Mishi is reluctant to discuss it with them for fear of appearing unintelligent in front of this team member and others. You know all of the following statements are true except which one? Choose the least correct answer.

    A. This demonstrates a lack of general management skills on Mishi's part.

    B. This demonstrates a lack of leadership skills on Mishi's part.

    C. This demonstrates a lack of communication skills on Mishi's part.

    D. This demonstrates a lack of product skills and knowledge on Mishi's part.

14. According to the Organizational Planning process, the role and responsibility of this project member is generally critical for most projects but may differ depending on the application area or industry you're working in.

    A. Executive sponsor

    B. Key stakeholders

    C. Project manager

    D. Technical resources with specific expertise

15. When working in the Source Selection process, you might consider asking the vendor to supply you with an ink sample for a project you're working on. The ink must have special qualities (they were outlined in the RFQ) and before making a selection, you want to test the ink in the printers that will be used at project deployment. All of the following statements are true except for which one? Choose the least correct answer.

    A. This is an example of evaluation criteria, which is an output of Solicitation Planning.

    B. This is an example of evaluation criteria, which is an input of the Source Selection process.

    C. This is an example of evaluation criteria, which is always objective and is used to rate or score proposals.

    D. Evaluation criteria might also include financial capacity and technical capability.

16. You are the newly appointed project manager over a high-profile, critical project for your organization. The project team is structured outside your normal organizational structure, and you have full authority for this project. What type of organization does this describe?

    A. Composite

    B. Strong matrix

    C. Functional

    D. Balanced matrix

17. Your project includes a new manufacturing technique that requires knowledge of chemical engineering. The project team must have access to at least two full-time resources with these skills. You know all of the following statements are true except for which one?

    A. Skills and knowledge about the product of the project are a tool and technique of the Project Plan Development process.

    B. Skills are primarily identified in the Resource Planning process.

    C. Resources are provided through the Staff Acquisition process.

    D. Resource requirements should include what types of resources are needed and the quantity of resources needed for each work package level.

18. You've decided to put your project management skills to work at home. Your house needs painting and you decide to plan it out as a project, identifying all the activities and sequencing them correctly. After an inspection of the house, you decide the rain gutters should be replaced too. The painters have told you they cannot start painting until the crew replacing the gutters has installed the new gutters and cleaned up their work space. Once the gutter crew gives the painters a thumbs-up, they'll start painting. What is this an example of?
    A. A start-to-finish (SF) relationship, which is the only relationship ADM uses
    B. A finish-to-start (FS) relationship, which is the only relationship PDM uses
    C. A finish-to-start (FS) relationship, which is the only relationship ADM uses
    D. A start-to-finish (SF) relationship, which is the only relationship PDM uses

19. You work for a nonprofit organization and are currently heading up a project to bring clean drinking water to several villages on a remote island in South America. This island has recently been at civil war, and there is concern that civil unrest may erupt during the implementation phase of this project. All of the following statements are true regarding this question except for which one? Choose the least correct answer.
    A. This risk poses a threat to the project objectives.
    B. This is a force majeure risk.
    C. This is an external risk.
    D. This is a performance risk.

20. Which of the following statements is true regarding qualified sellers lists?
    A. Qualified sellers lists are a tool and technique of the process concerned with obtaining responses to RFPs from vendors.
    B. Qualified sellers lists are a tool and technique of the process concerned with the receipt of bids and proposals.
    C. Qualified sellers lists are an input of the process concerned with obtaining responses to RFPs from vendors.
    D. Qualified sellers lists are an input of the process concerned with the receipt of bids and proposals.

21. Given the following information, is the project schedule ahead or behind what was planned for this period? EV = 95, PV = 85, AC = 100.
    A. Ahead, because the result of the variance formula is negative.
    B. Behind, because the result of the variance formula is negative.
    C. Ahead, because the result of the variance formula is positive.
    D. Behind, because the result of the variance formula is positive.

22. You work for a nonprofit organization in your local community. Your project will establish a new community outreach program for preteens. This project is being funded by a grant awarded to your organization based on its innovative ideas and approach. The project has consumed more financial resources than originally anticipated, so you've written and submitted a request for additional grant money to continue with the project. Today you received word that the grant has been denied. All of the following statements are true except:

    A. This project came about as a result of a social need.
    B. Cost overruns should have been identified when performance measures were taken.
    C. This project ended due to extinction.
    D. Corrective action should have been put into place to keep the project on track with the plan and the budget.

23. The project plan is used in several ways during the course of the project. All of the following involve uses for the project plan except:

    A. To guide the Project Plan Execution process
    B. As historical information for future projects of similar nature
    C. To help determine the project budget
    D. To support communications among stakeholders and the project team

24. Which of the following statements is *not* true regarding problem solving?

    A. Problem definition should focus on separating causes and symptoms.
    B. Decision making involves asking questions to determine if the issues are internal or external.
    C. Problem solving is a two-step process involving problem definition and decision making.
    D. Decision making has a timing element.

25. You are in the process of attaining and hiring resources for the project. Some of the resources can be found from within the organization, but three of the resources you've identified must be hired on contract. You need to consider previous experience, personal interests, personal characteristics, availability, and competencies and proficiency of the contractors as well as the internal staff. Which of the following statements is the best answer?

    A. The situation in this question refers to the staffing pool description, which is an input to the Resource Planning process.
    B. The situation in this question refers to staffing requirements, which are an output of Resource Planning.
    C. The situation in this question refers to the staffing requirements, which are an output of Staff Acquisition.
    D. The situation in this question refers to the staffing pool description, which is an input to the Staff Acquisition process.

26. According to *A Guide to the PMBOK*, scope changes, cost, resources, assignments, schedule changes, and so on are just a few of the items that may require this general management skill during the life cycle of your next project.

   A. Negotiation
   B. Influencing
   C. Problem solving
   D. Communicating

27. According to *A Guide to the PMBOK*, all of the following are terms for a contract except:

   A. Purchase order
   B. Memorandum of understanding
   C. Agreement
   D. Procurement order

28. You are a project manager working on contract for an upscale retail toy store. Your project involves implementing a Party Event Planner department in stores in 12 locations across the country as a pilot to determine if this will be a profitable new service all the stores should offer. You've identified two alternative methods of implementing the pilot. Alternative A's initial investment equals $598,000. The PV of the expected cash inflows is $300,000 in year 1 and $300,000 in year 2. The cost of capital is 12 percent. Alternative B's initial investment equals $625,000. The PV of the Alternative B's expected cash inflows is $323,000 in year 1 and $300,000 in year 2. The cost of capital is 9 percent. Which of the following is true?

   A. Alternative A will earn a return of at least 12 percent.
   B. Alternative B will earn a return of at least 9 percent.
   C. The return is not known for either Alternative A or Alternative B.
   D. Both alternatives are viable choices.

29. You work for Writer's Block, a service that reviews and critiques manuscripts for aspiring writers. You were assigned to be the project manager for a brand new computer system that logs, tracks, and electronically scans and files all submitted manuscripts along with the editor's notes. You hired and worked with a vendor who wrote the system from scratch to your specifications. You are in the Closing processes, and you're reviewing a report regarding certain aspects of the project's performance. The report states the following, "The reviewers recommend that future projects of this nature use a separate RFP process to acquire hardware." Which of the following options contains this information, given the circumstances in this question? Choose the best answer.

   A. Lessons learned
   B. Performance measurements documentation
   C. Procurement audit
   D. None of the answers given are correct.

30. You are working on determining activity start and finish dates, and you prefer using the method that allows for multiple time estimates as opposed to using the most likely estimate. Which of the following statements is true?

    A. You are using the PERT method to calculate start and finish dates. The PERT method differs from CPM in that PERT uses expected value to determine activity start and finish dates, whereas CPM uses most likely estimates to determine start and finish dates.

    B. You are using the CPM method to calculate start and finish dates, because this method allows for multiple time estimates.

    C. You are using the PERT method to calculate start and finish dates, which uses the most likely estimate to determine start and finish dates.

    D. You are using the GERT method to calculate start and finish dates, because this method allows for multiple time estimates.

31. You are managing a project for a grocery retail distributor, and the project is well underway. You are using an integrating methodology that both helps integrate the project processes and measures project performance. What integrating methodology are you using?

    A. EVM
    B. CPM
    C. EV
    D. EON

32. If EV = 145, PV = 162, AC = 138, BAC = 200, and ETC = 62, what is VAC? Assume past estimating assumptions are no longer valid.

    A. 0
    B. 7
    C. 9.5
    D. 62

33. You are a project manager for Time Will Tell, an international watch manufacturer. Your project entails developing a watch with global positioning satellite (GPS) capabilities. Kit is a junior staff member with two years of experience in GPS technology. Carrie is a senior staff member with five years of experience working GPS technology. You are developing the activity duration estimates for the project activities. You are trying to determine an estimate for a particular activity that involves GPS skills and knowledge. Carrie has worked on activities similar to this in the past. She tells you the activity will likely take 45 days. All of the following statements are true regarding the information in this question except:

   A. Carrie used an analogous estimating technique to come up with the 45-day estimate for this activity.

   B. The activities are similar in fact, not just appearance, and Carrie has the needed expertise to provide this estimate so you can rely on the estimate being reasonably accurate.

   C. Carrie used a technique that is a form of expert judgment to estimate this activity.

   D. The technique Carrie used can also be used to estimate project duration, because there is a lot of information available about the details of the project.

34. You are a project manager working on a project that involves developing a prototype packaging system that will allow perishable food items to sit on the shelf. The project is still in the beginning phases, and you know that some project risks may not have been identified yet. Changes will occur as the project progresses, and new risks may come to light or previously identified risks may take on new consequences as the project proceeds. Which of the following statements is true regarding this question? Choose the best answer.

   A. This question describes the project status input to the Qualitative Risk Analysis process and supports the idea that Qualitative Risk Analysis should be performed throughout the life of the project.

   B. The statements made in this question support the idea that Quantitative Risk Analysis should be performed throughout the life of the project.

   C. This question describes the importance of Risk Management Planning, because new risks will come to light as the project progresses and the risk management plan addresses how these risks should be managed once discovered.

   D. This question describes the project type input to the Quantitative Risk Analysis process and supports the idea that the type of project affects the occurrence of the risk events, depending on the life cycle phase of the project.

**35.** This is the first project you've managed using your company's new project management software. You are impressed with its performance and capabilities. You are also using EVM techniques. What knowledge area are you performing?

   **A.** Project Scope Management
   **B.** Project Time Management
   **C.** Project Integration Management
   **D.** Project Communications Management

**36.** Your project is being performed under contract. A scope change has occurred. Which of the following tools and techniques are required to comply with contract terms and provisions?

   **A.** Project management information system
   **B.** Change control system
   **C.** Scope change control
   **D.** Acceptance decisions

**37.** You are a project manager for Wedding Planners, Inc. Since every wedding is unique, your organization believes in managing each one as a project. You've come up with a great idea for a new event that you're certain customers will love that will also profit the company. Your boss asks you to investigate alternative methods for implementing the new idea and come back with a recommendation. You discover that Alternative A could yield revenues of $98,000 over the next two years, while Alternative B could yield revenues of $105,000 over three years. The finance manager told you to use eight percent as the cost of capital. Which project should you choose and why?

   **A.** Alternative A, because the discounted cash flows are $84,019, while the discounted cash flows for Alternative B are $83,352.
   **B.** Alternative B, because its yield is higher than Alternative A's yield.
   **C.** Alternative B, because the discounted cash flows are $84,019, while the discounted cash flows for Alternative A are $83,352.
   **D.** Alternative A, because the discounted cash flows are $96,457, while the discounted cash flows for Alternative B are $84,677.

**38.** Which of the following project management knowledge area involves every team member and stakeholder on the project?

   **A.** Project Scope Management
   **B.** Project Communications Management
   **C.** Project Human Resources Management
   **D.** Project Quality Management

39. You are working on a research and development project in the agriculture industry. Your risk management team has identified several risks and has determined that the most significant risk to the project is a financial risk. The most effective response for this type of risk is:

    A. Avoidance

    B. Acceptance

    C. Mitigation

    D. Transference

40. Initial project costs can be broken down into three areas. Which of the following is *not* true regarding the initial project budget and the identification of these project costs?

    A. Either the project manager or a functional manager may have the responsibility of identifying project costs.

    B. The three areas of project costs are human resources costs, resource or project costs, and administrative costs. Depending on the project, either human resource costs or project costs may be the largest project costs.

    C. Functional managers external to the project typically manage project budgets when the resource or project costs are the largest expense of the project.

    D. Consider historical information, previous projects of similar scope, stakeholders, and key team members when determining initial project costs.

41. You are a project manager for a new Information Technology project. Your organization requires you to organize the project according to project phases common to programming projects (initiation, requirements gathering, design, code, test, and implement). Once requirements are gathered, the major deliverables of the project will be finalized. You're in the Scope Definition process, and you know that which of the following statements is true?

    A. The project itself is always the first level of decomposition, followed by the major deliverables and the constituent components.

    B. The project phases should be the first level of decomposition, and the major deliverables should be the second level of decomposition.

    C. The major deliverables should be the first level of decomposition, followed by the constituent components of the deliverables.

    D. The project phases are not part of the decomposition process but rather an organization method for the work of the project.

42. You are a project manager for Rhone Valley importers. Your buyer has found a new product that she's convinced will sell well in this country. Taking on this new product introduces considerable opportunity for the company, but at the same time is also a considerable threat. The cost of this product exceeds anything your company has imported before, and if it doesn't sell as well as the buyer thinks it will, the company could go into bankruptcy. You think through the next steps and determine that all of the following statements are true except for which one?
    A. Conduct a feasibility study to determine the potential market, costs, risks, and other factors.
    B. One purpose of the feasibility study is to determine. marketing demand for the new product that could in turn become the demand that drives the project.
    C. During the feasibility study, you could use the Project Risk Management processes to identify all opportunities and exploit their possibilities, and determine the potential threats and minimize their probability and consequences.
    D. One of the end results of the feasibility study might be to produce a project overview that will include a description of the intended outcome of the project, a list of the project deliverables, and a detailed project schedule for management review.

43. Which of the following best describes a project constraint?
    A. Customer request
    B. Product description
    C. Management directive
    D. Cost baseline

44. You are working on a research and development project in the agriculture industry. Your risk management team has identified several risks and has determined that the most significant risk to the project is a quality risk. You've identified a strategy to deal with this risk, but the risk management team agrees it may not be effective. What is the best action you should take given this situation?
    A. Accept the risk.
    B. Develop a fallback plan.
    C. Develop a contingency plan.
    D. Establish a contingency allowance.

45. Which of the following best describes a project assumption?
    A. The equipment needed for the second deliverable of the project will be delivered one week prior to the start of the work for this deliverable.
    B. The project's allotted budget is $425,000, but you know this is only a rough estimate and will be changed as the project plan is further developed.
    C. Organizational structure
    D. Project schedule

**46.** You are a project manager for Wedding Planners, Inc. Since every wedding is unique, your organization believes in managing each one as a project. You've come up with a great idea for a new event that you're certain customers will love that will also profit the company. Your boss asks you to investigate alternative methods for implementing the new idea and come back with a recommendation. You discover that Alternative A could yield revenues of $98,000 over the next two years and has an IRR of eight percent. Alternative B could yield revenues of $105,000 over three years and has an IRR of six percent. Which project should you choose and why?

**A.** Alternative A, because it has higher revenues in a shorter amount of time.

**B.** Alternative A, because it has a higher IRR than Alternative B.

**C.** Alternative B, because it has higher revenues overall.

**D.** There isn't enough information in the question to determine an answer.

**47.** Your project sponsor has requested a cost estimate for the project you're working on. This project is similar in scope to a project you worked on last year. She would like to get the cost estimates as soon as possible. Accuracy is not her primary concern right now. She needs a ballpark figure by tomorrow. You decide to use

**A.** Analogous estimating techniques

**B.** Bottom-up estimating techniques

**C.** Parametric modeling techniques

**D.** Computerized modeling techniques

**48.** You are the project manager for BB Tops, a nationwide toy store chain. You are working on estimates for your latest project and have gathered several variables for your model. You've determined which of the following?

**A.** Parametric modeling is a top-down technique that uses variables to produce time estimates.

**B.** Parametric modeling is a mathematical formula that uses variables to produce cost estimates.

**C.** Contingency estimating is a top-down technique that uses variables to produce cost estimates.

**D.** Contingency estimating is a mathematical model that uses variables to produce time estimates.

**49.** Your team members have turned in their activity estimates. Hugh's activity will take 30 days; Leah's activity will take 15 days; and Destiny's activity will take 60 days. Leah also gives you an updated description of her activity because the current description is not correct. Each of them is experienced with the activity they've been assigned and used their previous experience with a similar activity as their basis for this estimate. Which of the following actions will you perform based on the information in this question? Choose the best answer.

**A.** Update the WBS.

**B.** Create the Activity Duration Estimate output for each activity and record the estimates as they were given to you.

**C.** Document the assumptions made about the estimating process as part of the supporting detail output to this process.

**D.** Update the activity list as required.

**50.** You are the project manager for a new website for the local zoo. You need to perform Quantitative Risk Analysis. You'll use all of the following tools and techniques to accomplish this except:

   **A.** Data precision ranking

   **B.** Sensitivity analysis

   **C.** Decision tree analysis

   **D.** Interviewing

**51.** You work for a nonprofit organization and are currently heading up a project to bring clean drinking water to several villages on a remote island in South America. Your stakeholders have changed the scope of this project three times already, and the steering committee has reprioritized this project twice during the last six months. Which of the following risk categories does this represent?

   **A.** Quality risk

   **B.** Organizational risk

   **C.** Project management risk

   **D.** External risk

**52.** If EV = 145, PV = 162, AC = 138, BAC = 200, and ETC = 62, what is ETC? Assume that current variances are not typical.

   **A.** 7

   **B.** 55

   **C.** 62

   **D.** 9.6

**53.** Why is assessing risk probability in the Qualitative Risk Analysis process difficult? Choose the best answer.

   **A.** Because it relies on historical data.

   **B.** Because the values are cardinal.

   **C.** Because the values are ordinal.

   **D.** Because it relies on expert judgment.

**54.** You are examining the network paths for your project. Path A's duration is: 1-2-3-5-8; Path B's duration is 1-3-5-6-7; Path C's duration is 1-2-5-4-9; and Path D's duration is 2-3-4-4-8. Which of the following is the critical path for this project?

   **A.** Path D

   **B.** Path C

   **C.** Path B

   **D.** Path A

**55.** Which of the following statements is *not* true regarding the technique of benefit/cost analysis in the Scope Planning process?

  **A.** Benefit/cost analysis may incorporate several financial measures—including return on investment and payback period—to determine the attractiveness of various alternatives.

  **B.** Benefit/cost analysis estimates the tangible and intangible costs and benefits of product alternatives.

  **C.** Benefit/cost analysis estimates the tangible and intangible costs and benefits of project alternatives.

  **D.** Benefit/cost analysis may incorporate several financial measures—including return on investment and payback period—to determine the baseline for cost measurement control.

**56.** You are a project manager who works for a nationwide bank with branches in every major city in the country. You are working on creating a project plan. Your project entails introducing a new home equity loan product to the bank customers. You realize that since you work for a bank, the financial policies in your organization are fairly strict. Throughout the course of your project you'll need to make certain you adhere to these policies. All of the following statements are true regarding this project except for which of the following?

  **A.** Organizational policies are an input to the Project Plan Development process.

  **B.** You should consider the personnel policies and quality policies of your organization as well as the financial policies.

  **C.** You should consider other planning outputs when working on the project plan. They include all of the outputs from all of the core processes in the Planning process group.

  **D.** Constraints and assumptions are not to be overlooked. Like many processes in the Planning process group, these are inputs to the Project Plan Development process.

**57.** Your team is in the performing stage of team development. The following exchange took place at your last team meeting: "I'm glad you're all having fun, but it's time to get down to business," you say. "I'd like to introduce Sunny Knight. He'll be taking over for Cheri, who you all know is out on maternity leave." Which of the following statements is true?

  **A.** A new team member has been introduced, which means the team development stages will start all over the forming stage.

  **B.** A new team member has been introduced, which means the team development stages start over with the conforming stage.

  **C.** A new team member has been introduced, which means the team development stages start over with compromise stage.

  **D.** The team was in the performing stage and will stay in this stage, even though a new team member has been introduced.

**58.** Your manager storms into your office demanding to know what paragraph three of the recent status report means, even though she clearly knows what it means by the tone in her voice. She wants you to know that, after all, she is the Director of Marketing and has the authority to "do what it takes" to keep you in line. She doesn't appreciate your mention of the items in paragraph three and tells you if you do it again, she'll take further action to make sure you're demoted. Which type of power does your manager practice? Choose the best answer.

   **A.** Referent

   **B.** Punishment

   **C.** Social

   **D.** Confrontation

**59.** Given the following information, are the costs of the project higher than budgeted or lower than budgeted? EV = 85, PV = 95, AC = 100.

   **A.** Lower than budgeted, because the result of the variance formula is negative.

   **B.** Higher than budgeted, because the result of the variance formula is negative.

   **C.** Higher than budgeted, because the result of the variance formula is positive.

   **D.** Lower than budgeted, because the result of the variance formula is positive.

**60.** This tool and technique of the Schedule Control process is the key factor in controlling the time constraint.

   **A.** Performance measurement

   **B.** Variance analysis

   **C.** Additional planning

   **D.** Trend analysis

**61.** The last phase of your project is the testing phase. Two teams of testers are responsible for checking the product your project has produced to be certain it works correctly prior to delivery to the customer. What is this an example of?

   **A.** Trending

   **B.** Inspection

   **C.** Tolerance

   **D.** Prevention

**62.** You work in the pharmaceutical industry, and your organization has decided to build a new laboratory facility in the Northwest. Marketing demand is driving new research for diet medications, and the new lab will be dedicated to this product development project. The building project is a separate project from the diet drug research, but the diet drug research cannot be conducted until the building is complete. The building project was contracted out to a vendor and is scheduled for completion within the next three weeks. You begin the Administrative Closure process and know that this process entails all of the following tasks except:

   **A.** Ensuring that the project records accurately reflect the building specifications

   **B.** Analyzing the project management process for effectiveness

   **C.** Updating the roles and responsibility documentation

   **D.** Verifying and accepting the product documentation

**63.** You are a project manager and are in the Closing processes of the project. Your customer has been presented with a formal acceptance and sign-off document. They refuse to sign, claiming the product does not meet their expectations. You know that this situation could have been prevented by doing all of the following except:

   **A.** Documenting the requirements

   **B.** Documenting the customer's refusal to sign

   **C.** Performing quality inspections during the process

   **D.** Requesting sign-off at important milestones

**64.** Which of the following statements best describes the purpose of the Scope Planning process?

   **A.** To progressively elaborate, document, and assign project roles and responsibilities to the project work that produces the product of the project.

   **B.** To progressively elaborate and document the project scope that produces the product of the project.

   **C.** To progressively elaborate the work of the project so that baselines for performance measurement and controls can be established.

   **D.** To progressively elaborate and document the deliverables of the project, determine adequate cost and duration estimates, and identify constituent components of the product of the project.

# Answers to Final Exam Reviews 1-4

# Answers to Final Exam Review 1

1. C. The formula to calculate lines of communication is: $(n \times (n-1)) \div 2$. If you plug 22 attendees into this formula, you find that there are 231 lines of communication. $(22 \times (22-1)) \div 2 = 231$. Most groups make effective decisions when there are between 5 and 11 members. For more information, see Chapter 8 of Sybex's *PMP: Project Management Professional Study Guide*, 2nd Edition.

2. D. Mathematical analysis is a tool and technique of the Schedule Development process that calculates potential dates for activities. These dates are not the project schedule; they are the potential dates the activities can be scheduled given constraints and resource limitations. For more information, see Chapter 7 of Sybex's *PMP: Project Management Professional Study Guide*, 2nd Edition.

3. D. The EAC formula for this question is AC + ETC. Plugging in the numbers from the question, you get 138 + 62 = 200. For more information, see Chapter 9 of Sybex's *PMP: Project Management Professional Study Guide*, 2nd Edition.

4. B. Project selection methods are a tool and technique of Initiation and can be used to choose which projects the organization should undertake or to choose among alternative ways of doing a project. Project selection criteria (an input to Initiation) concern the things executive managers typically think about such as financial return, customer loyalty, public perception, and so on. For more information, see Chapter 3 of Sybex's *PMP: Project Management Professional Study Guide*, 2nd Edition.

5. D. Programs are groups of projects managed collectively to gain benefits that couldn't be gained by managing them separately. For more information, see Chapter 1 of Sybex's *PMP: Project Management Professional Study Guide*, 2nd Edition.

6. C. Project risk response audits are concerned with the implementation and effective use of the transference, avoidance, and mitigation risk strategies. For more information, see Chapter 10 of Sybex's *PMP: Project Management Professional Study Guide*, 2nd Edition.

7. C. Project management software is a tool and technique of Resource Planning and is used to help organize resource pools. Cost Estimating mentions project management software's ability to help with cost estimating under the tool and technique called computerized tools. It's mentioned in the PDM tool and technique of Activity Sequencing and implied in the ADM method. Project management software is also mentioned in the information retrieval systems tool and technique of the Information Distribution process. For more information, see Chapter 5 of Sybex's *PMP: Project Management Professional Study Guide*, 2nd Edition.

8. B. When project team members are identified in the project charter, this is known as preassignment, which is a tool and technique of Staff Acquisition. For more information, see Chapter 5 of Sybex's *PMP: Project Management Professional Study Guide*, 2nd Edition.

9. D. The risk management plan does not address responses to individual risks. For more information, see Chapter 6 of Sybex's *PMP: Project Management Professional Study Guide*, 2nd Edition.

**10.** A. The forecast of the likely total costs of the project is the estimate at completion (EAC) formula, which is an output of the Cost Control process. For more information, see Chapter 10 of Sybex's *PMP: Project Management Professional Study Guide*, 2nd Edition.

**11.** D. Triangular distributions rely on optimistic, pessimistic, and most likely estimates to determine risk ratings. For more information, see Chapter 6 of Sybex's *PMP: Project Management Professional Study Guide*, 2nd Edition.

**12.** D. The terms bid and quotation are typically used when you're basing selection decisions on price. The organization probably is looking for a fixed price contract, but the question is asking what criteria the source selection is based on. For more information, see Chapter 6 of Sybex's *PMP: Project Management Professional Study Guide*, 2nd Edition.

**13.** A. CPI = EV ÷ AC; therefore, 114 ÷ 103 = 1.1. SPI = EV ÷ PV; therefore, 114 ÷ 120 = .95. For more information, see Chapter 9 of Sybex's *PMP: Project Management Professional Study Guide*, 2nd Edition.

**14.** A. Technical performance measurements compares the technical accomplishments of project milestones completed during the Executing processes to the technical milestones defined in the project Planning process. For more information, see Chapter 10 of Sybex's *PMP: Project Management Professional Study Guide*, 2nd Edition.

**15.** B. While phase exits are a good idea for vendor projects, they are not required. For more information, see Chapter 1 of Sybex's *PMP: Project Management Professional Study Guide*, 2nd Edition.

**16.** C. Quality Control is the process concerned with correctness of the work, while Scope Verification is the process concerned with acceptance of the work. For more information, see Chapter 9 of Sybex's *PMP: Project Management Professional Study Guide*, 2nd Edition.

**17.** A. Imposed dates and key events constraints are two categories of time constraints that should be taken into consideration when examining the constraints input to the Schedule Development process. For more information, see Chapter 7 of Sybex's *PMP: Project Management Professional Study Guide*, 2nd Edition.

**18.** D. NPV allows you to calculate an accurate value for each project. In order to determine NPV, you must calculate the PV of the cash flows for each alternative and subtract the initial investment from the sum of the present value of the cash flows. Alternative A's NPV is <571>, Alternative B's NPV is 6,620, and Alternative C's NPV is 1,165. Based on these criteria alone, either alternative B or C is an acceptable choice. The calculations for each alternative are as follows: Alternative A's year 1 PV = 12,727 and year 2 PV = 15,702, for a total of 28,429. Alternative B's year 1 PV = 19,091 and year 2 PV = 16,529, for a total of 35,620. Alternative C's year 1 PV = 13,636 and year 2 PV = 16,529, for a total of 30,165. For more information, see Chapter 3 of Sybex's *PMP: Project Management Professional Study Guide*, 2nd Edition.

**19.** A. Quality Control does not have a change control system tool and technique. For more information, see Chapter 10 of Sybex's *PMP: Project Management Professional Study Guide*, 2nd Edition.

**20.** C. The triple constraints are time, money, and quality and are usually present on all projects. Most likely, one or two of these constraints will be the primary driver on a project. Constraints other than the triple constraints will be present on most projects. Answer D is incorrect, because the organizational structure does not impact the way you manage or deal with constraints. For more information, see Chapter 1 of Sybex's *PMP: Project Management Professional Study Guide*, 2nd Edition.

**21.** C. WBSs from previous projects can be used as templates on projects that are producing similar products or services. Some companies write WBS templates to be used for projects of similar scope. For more information, see Chapter 4 of Sybex's *PMP: Project Management Professional Study Guide*, 2nd Edition.

**22.** C. The CDs included with the books are considered intellectual property and should not be copied, no matter if you're a PMP or not. For more information, see Chapter 12 of Sybex's *PMP: Project Management Professional Study Guide*, 2nd Edition.

**23.** C. The tools and techniques for Activity Duration Estimating are expert judgment, analogous estimating, quantitatively based durations, and reserve time. For more information, see Chapter 5 of Sybex's *PMP: Project Management Professional Study Guide*, 2nd Edition.

**24.** C. Decomposition includes identifying major deliverables, determining adequate cost and duration estimates, identifying constituent components, and verifying correctness of decomposition. For more information, see Chapter 4 of Sybex's *PMP: Project Management Professional Study Guide*, 2nd Edition.

**25.** D. First, you must determine expected value. The expected value formula is:

(Optimistic + Pessimistic + (4 × Most Likely)) ÷ 6

The formula for this question is:

(245 + 269 + (4 × 257)) ÷ 6 = 257

Next, you need to determine the standard deviation. Standard deviation is calculated as:

(Pessimistic − Optimistic) ÷ 6

The formula for this question is:

(269 − 245) ÷ 6 = 4

95 percent confidence level is determined by adding and subtracting two standard deviations to the expected value. Therefore, the range of dates for this question is 249 days to 265 days. For more information, see Chapter 7 of Sybex's *PMP: Project Management Professional Study Guide*, 2nd Edition.

**26.** A. The PI matrix can be developed using cardinal or ordinal scales. It is a tool and technique of the Qualitative Risk Analysis process. For more information, see Chapter 6 of Sybex's *PMP: Project Management Professional Study Guide*, 2nd Edition.

**27.** C. The tools and techniques of Activity Duration Estimating are expert judgment, analogous estimating, quantitatively based durations, and reserve time (contingency). For more information, see Chapter 5 of Sybex's *PMP: Project Management Professional Study Guide*, 2nd Edition.

**28.** B. Project Plan Execution is where the work of the project is performed. Activities are clarified, the work is authorized to begin, and resources are committed to the project and perform the work. For more information, see Chapter 8 of Sybex's *PMP: Project Management Professional Study Guide*, 2nd Edition.

**29.** C. Negotiation is working with others to come to an agreement. Arbitration and mediation are two forms of negotiation. For more information, see Chapter 1 of Sybex's *PMP: Project Management Professional Study Guide*, 2nd Edition.

**30.** B. A proper change control system documents the procedures a project manager can use to approve changes in an emergency. Answer B states that this procedure is documented, so you have the authority to approve the change. For more information, see Chapter 10 of Sybex's *PMP: Project Management Professional Study Guide*, 2nd Edition.

**31.** C. Both Alternative A and Alternative C yield a positive NPV, so either project may be chosen based on this criteria alone. For more information, see Chapter 3 of Sybex's *PMP: Project Management Professional Study Guide*, 2nd Edition.

**32.** C. The collective phases a project progresses through are known as the project life cycle. For more information, see Chapter 1 of Sybex's *PMP: Project Management Professional Study Guide*, 2nd Edition.

**33.** C. Quality improvements are an output of the Quality Control process and the Quality Assurance process and come about as a result of quality audits. They may help improve efficiency or effectiveness on the project, thereby increasing the value of the project and exceeding stakeholder expectations. Identifying lessons learned is the objective of quality audits, not quality improvements. For more information, see Chapter 9 of Sybex's *PMP: Project Management Professional Study Guide*, 2nd Edition.

**34.** A. Mandatory dependencies are also known as hard logic and are related to the nature of the work being done. They often involve physical limitations. In this question, no new construction activity can begin until the demolition activity is completed so demolition is a mandatory dependency. For more information, see Chapter 5 of Sybex's *PMP: Project Management Professional Study Guide*, 2nd Edition.

**35.** A. The Hygiene Theory says salary isn't a motivator unless there are large disparities in salary. For more information, see Chapter 8 of Sybex's *PMP: Project Management Professional Study Guide*, 2nd Edition.

**36.** A. The Initiation process is characterized by low costs, low staffing levels, decreased chances for a successful completion, high risk, and the greatest amount of stakeholder influence concerning the characteristics of the product or service of the project. Initiation acknowledges that the project or next phase of the project should begin and authorizes the assignment of resources. For more information, see Chapter 1 of Sybex's *PMP: Project Management Professional Study Guide*, 2nd Edition.

**37.** D. It would be inappropriate to send the prospective client a gift basket. This option constitutes conflict of interest in the hopes of personal gain. For more information, see Chapter 12 of Sybex's *PMP: Project Management Professional Study Guide*, 2nd Edition.

**38.** C. Parametric modeling, according to *A Guide to the PMBOK*, requires parameters that are easily quantifiable, historical information that's accurate, and a model that's scalable. Resources may need expertise but option C belongs with the analogous estimating technique. For more information, see Chapter 5 of Sybex's *PMP: Project Management Professional Study Guide*, 2nd Edition.

**39.** D. Project Time Management allows for the combining of Activity Sequencing, Activity Duration Estimating, and Schedule Development processes into one process that can be completed by one person. For more information, see Chapter 2 of Sybex's *PMP: Project Management Professional Study Guide*, 2nd Edition.

**40.** A. Project 1's payback period is 20 months. Year 1 inflows are $204,000. Year 2 inflows for the first 8 months are $96,000, making the payback period 20 months. Project 2's payback period is 25 months. Year 1 inflows are $176,000. Year 2 inflows are 144,000, and an additional month at $12,000 makes the payback period 25 months. For more information, see Chapter 3 of Sybex's *PMP: Project Management Professional Study Guide*, 2nd Edition.

**41.** B. Thresholds are used to measure the project team's effectiveness at executing risk response plans. For more information, see Chapter 6 of Sybex's *PMP: Project Management Professional Study Guide*, 2nd Edition.

**42.** C. The WBS dictionary contains information such as the schedule dates, staff assignments, and cost budgets. For more information, see Chapter 4 of Sybex's *PMP: Project Management Professional Study Guide*, 2nd Edition.

**43.** A. Value Engineering is a technique used to help improve project schedules, profits, quality, and resource usage, and it optimizes life-cycle costs. For more information, see Chapter 2 of Sybex's *PMP: Project Management Professional Study Guide*, 2nd Edition.

**44.** B. The processes in the Project Procurement Management knowledge area are considered from the perspective of the buyer. Goals as well as deliverables should be measurable. For more information, see Chapter 2 of Sybex's *PMP: Project Management Professional Study Guide*, 2nd Edition.

**45.** A. The Initiation process has just begun, and the inputs to this process are product description, strategic plan, project selection criteria, and historical information. The project charter is not produced until the end of the Initiation process. For more information, see Chapter 2 of Sybex's *PMP: Project Management Professional Study Guide*, 2nd Edition.

**46.** C. The project objectives should include quantifiable criteria that can be used to help measure project success. Project objectives should always include schedule, cost, and quality measurements. For more information, see Chapter 4 of Sybex's *PMP: Project Management Professional Study Guide*, 2nd Edition.

**47.** A. Both the Contract Closeout and the Administrative Closure processes should be performed. The contract is complete, which requires the Contract Closeout process, and the project phase is complete. Administrative Closure is performed when project phases are completed. For more information, see Chapter 11 of Sybex's *PMP: Project Management Professional Study Guide*, 2nd Edition.

**48.** C. Answer C describes project selection methods that are concerned with measuring the value and benefits of the project. Project selection criteria are concerned with the advantages or merits of the product of the project to the organization. For more information, see Chapter 3 of Sybex's *PMP: Project Management Professional Study Guide*, 2nd Edition.

**49.** C. Weighted scoring models use the weight of the criteria multiplied by the score to derive an overall score. Project 1's score is 47, Project 2's score is 45, and Project 3's score is 42. Based on this information, Project 1 is the best choice. For more information, see Chapter 3 of Sybex's *PMP: Project Management Professional Study Guide*, 2nd Edition.

**50.** D. This question indicates that you are in the Executing process and have a problem on your hands that needs immediate attention. While you absolutely should report the risk trigger and the actions you took at the next stakeholder meeting, it isn't something you'd do immediately, as the question indicates. For more information, see Chapter 8 of Sybex's *PMP: Project Management Professional Study Guide*, 2nd Edition.

**51.** C. Loaning the book and CD to your friend is an acceptable solution as long as your friend does not make copies of the CD or printed text. For more information, see Chapter 12 of Sybex's *PMP: Project Management Professional Study Guide*, 2nd Edition.

**52.** C. Resource requirements, which help determine the number of resources required and what quantity is needed, are an output of the Resource Planning process. Organizational Planning's role and responsibility assignment output concerns assigning project roles and responsibilities to project stakeholders. For more information, see Chapter 5 of Sybex's *PMP: Project Management Professional Study Guide*, 2nd Edition.

**53.** B. The primary cost of meeting quality requirements for a project are the expenses incurred while performing project quality management activities, not just the tools and techniques of the process. For more information, see Chapter 6 of Sybex's *PMP: Project Management Professional Study Guide*, 2nd Edition.

**54.** A. The Risk Identification outputs are risks, triggers, and inputs to other processes. For more information, see Chapter 6 of Sybex's *PMP: Project Management Professional Study Guide*, 2nd Edition.

**55.** A. Monte Carlo analysis is a simulation tool and technique of this process. For more information, see Chapter 6 of Sybex's *PMP: Project Management Professional Study Guide*, 2nd Edition.

**56.** A. First, you must determine expected value. That formula is:

(Optimistic + Pessimistic + (4 × Most Likely)) ÷ 6

The formula for this question is:

(108 + 126 + (4 × 114)) ÷ 6 = 115

Next, you need to determine the standard deviation. Standard deviation is calculated as:

(Pessimistic – Optimistic) ÷ 6

The standard deviation formula for this question is:

(126 – 108) ÷ 6 = 3

The 68 percent confidence level is determined by adding and subtracting one standard deviation to the expected value. Therefore, the range of dates for this question is 112 days to 118 days. For more information, see Chapter 7 of Sybex's *PMP: Project Management Professional Study Guide*, 2nd Edition.

**57.** C. 99 percent confidence level is determined by adding and subtracting three standard deviations to the expected value. Therefore, the range of dates for this question is 585 days to 669 days. For more information, see Chapter 7 of Sybex's *PMP: Project Management Professional Study Guide*, 2nd Edition.

**58.** B. According to *A Guide to the PMBOK*, Team Development is performed throughout the project, not just during the Executing processes. For more information, see Chapter 8 of Sybex's *PMP: Project Management Professional Study Guide*, 2nd Edition.

**59.** B. Salary is no longer a motivator. Once a need has been met, it can no longer be a motivator. For more information, see Chapter 8 of Sybex's *PMP: Project Management Professional Study Guide*, 2nd Edition.

**60.** A. Confrontation is also called problem solving and should be the most commonly used technique by project managers. For more information, see Chapter 8 of Sybex's *PMP: Project Management Professional Study Guide*, 2nd Edition.

**61.** A. Modifications to deliverables, product changes, and termination for poor performance generate change requests, which are an input to the Contract Administration process. Answer C could be correct but is not the most correct answer. The "termination for poor performance" is the key statement in this question, which should lead you to the change request option. For more information, see Chapter 9 of Sybex's *PMP: Project Management Professional Study Guide*, 2nd Edition.

**62.** C. The earned value management (EVM) tool and technique continuously monitors and measures planned value (PV), earned value (EV), and actual costs (AC). For more information, see Chapter 10 of Sybex's *PMP: Project Management Professional Study Guide*, 2nd Edition.

**63.** B. Product documentation (an input of the Administrative Closure process) contains information regarding the product of the project. The scripts were developed by the project team and describe the product of the project. Therefore, they are considered product documentation. For more information, see Chapter 11 of Sybex's *PMP: Project Management Professional Study Guide*, 2nd Edition.

**64.** D. Historical information is not an input of the Scope Planning process. For more information, see Chapter 4 of Sybex's *PMP: Project Management Professional Study Guide*, 2nd Edition.

# Answers to Final Exam Review 2

1. B. Administrative Closure is part of the Project Communications Management knowledge area. For more information, see Chapter 11 of Sybex's *PMP: Project Management Professional Study Guide*, 2nd Edition.

2. B. The decomposition process does not assign unique identifiers at each level of the process. For more information, see Chapter 4 of Sybex's *PMP: Project Management Professional Study Guide*, 2nd Edition.

3. A. Design of experiments is an analytical technique that identifies the elements or variables that will have the greatest effect on overall project outcomes. For more information, see Chapter 6 of Sybex's *PMP: Project Management Professional Study Guide*, 2nd Edition.

4. A. Part of the *PMP Code of Professional Conduct* requires that you cooperate in any investigation concerning ethics violations and in collecting information related to the violation. For more information, see Chapter 12 of Sybex's *PMP: Project Management Professional Study Guide*, 2nd Edition.

5. D. This is an organizational procedure, which is a tool and technique of the Project Plan Execution process. Answer B could be correct except these actions occur in the Controlling process, not the Executing process. It's also possible, although not likely, that the paperwork and approvals could be accomplished by the end of the week in which case there may or may not be a variance. For more information, see Chapter 8 of Sybex's *PMP: Project Management Professional Study Guide*, 2nd Edition.

6. C. Conditional diagramming methods such as GERT and System Dynamics models allow for conditional branches and loops. For more information, see Chapter 5 of Sybex's *PMP: Project Management Professional Study Guide*, 2nd Edition.

7. A. Your boss is the project sponsor (who is also considered a stakeholder). The project sponsor is typically an executive in the organization that has the authority to assign resources and make critical decisions for the project. The VP of Sales is a stakeholder. This question also describes a composite organization. The organization is primarily a functional organization (the clues are the VP of Sales and VP of Marketing, who define a hierarchical structure found in functional organizations), but a project manager was assigned to run this critical project much like a projectized organization. For more information, see Chapter 1 of Sybex's *PMP: Project Management Professional Study Guide*, 2nd Edition.

8. B. The 80/20 rule was first observed by Pareto. The Pareto diagram—a histogram—is a tool and technique of the Quality Control process. For more information, see Chapter 10 of Sybex's *PMP: Project Management Professional Study Guide*, 2nd Edition.

9. C. Benefit measurement methods and constrained optimization methods are also known as decision models. They are a tool and technique of the Initiation process. For more information, see Chapter 3 of Sybex's *PMP: Project Management Professional Study Guide*, 2nd Edition.

**10.** B. Communication involves 90 percent of a project manager's time. For more information, see Chapter 8 of Sybex's *PMP: Project Management Professional Study Guide*, 2nd Edition.

**11.** C. Requisition is the contract life cycle phase where project objectives are refined, potential qualified vendors are reviewed, and solicitation materials are prepared. For more information, see Chapter 9 of Sybex's *PMP: Project Management Professional Study Guide*, 2nd Edition.

**12.** A. Remember that all questions on the exam will refer to specific terminology used in *A Guide to the PMBOK*. While answer B or C may seem correct, and in fact, might be the terms your organization uses, *A Guide to the PMBOK* calls this process phase exits, stage gates, or kill points. (See page 11 of *A Guide to the PMBOK*.) For more information, see Chapter 1 of Sybex's *PMP: Project Management Professional Study Guide*, 2nd Edition.

**13.** A. Negotiations are a tool and technique of the Staff Acquisition process. One of the inputs to Staff Acquisition—staffing pool description—will help you with the negotiation, because you should consider things such as competency levels, availability, and personal characteristics when negotiating with functional managers for resources. For more information, see Chapter 5 of Sybex's *PMP: Project Management Professional Study Guide*, 2nd Edition.

**14.** C. Contract documentation (an input of the Contract Closeout process) includes any technical documentation the vendor created as part of the project. This question states the vendor created the detailed technical specifications, which means this becomes part of the contract documentation. If the organization would have created the documentation themselves, this would be considered product documentation, which is an input of the Administrative Closure process. For more information, see Chapter 11 of Sybex's *PMP: Project Management Professional Study Guide*, 2nd Edition.

**15.** B. The activity duration estimates output is a quantitative assessment (not "qualitative" assessment as stated in answer B) of the likely number of work periods. This question is considering the capabilities of the resources ("Kit is a junior staff member," and "Carrie is a senior staff member," are your clues) and the resource requirements input. For more information, see Chapter 5 of Sybex's *PMP: Project Management Professional Study Guide*, 2nd Edition.

**16.** B. You haven't passed the exam yet, so it's unethical to put the PMP designation on your resume or application at this point in time. For more information, see Chapter 12 of Sybex's *PMP: Project Management Professional Study Guide*, 2nd Edition.

**17.** B. Imposed dates restrict the start date of activities with a "start no later than" date or finish date with a "finish no later than" date. Weather conditions are one example of imposed dates. Answer A and C are key events or major milestones, not imposed dates. For more information, see Chapter 7 of Sybex's *PMP: Project Management Professional Study Guide*, 2nd Edition.

**18.** B. Project closeout is an output of the Cost Control process that requires processes and procedures, and adherence to standards and regulations (where applicable depending on the industry) for closing out project costs. For more information, see Chapter 10 of Sybex's *PMP: Project Management Professional Study Guide*, 2nd Edition.

19. B. The question states you're working on the communications management plan, which rules out Answer D. Communications technology—an input to the Communications Planning process—considers the timing of the information or need for updates, the availability of the technology you're planning on using to communicate project information, the need to procure new technology or systems, staff experience, and the duration of the project. Each of these items are mentioned in this question, so the correct answer is B. For more information, see Chapter 4 of Sybex's *PMP: Project Management Professional Study Guide*, 2nd Edition.

20. D. When problems arise on a project, they should be resolved in favor of the customer whenever possible. This organization is a functional organization, as the department manager is responsible for assigning resources, which means the project manager has little authority or power. For more information, see Chapter 1 of Sybex's *PMP: Project Management Professional Study Guide*, 2nd Edition.

21. B. Quality audits are a tool and technique of the Quality Assurance process. For more information, see Chapter 9 of Sybex's *PMP: Project Management Professional Study Guide*, 2nd Edition.

22. D. Influencing entails the ability to get things done using power and politics. Power is the ability to get people to do things they wouldn't ordinarily do, and it's the ability to change minds and influence outcomes. Politics involve getting groups of people with diverse interests to cooperate creatively, even in the midst of conflict and disorder. For more information, see Chapter 1 of Sybex's *PMP: Project Management Professional Study Guide*, 2nd Edition.

23. A. Bottom-up estimating is a very accurate technique. The cost and accuracy of this process is related to the complexity and size of the project. Detailed project activities will result in accurate estimates and higher costs to perform this technique. For more information, see Chapter 5 of Sybex's *PMP: Project Management Professional Study Guide*, 2nd Edition.

24. B. Estimate to complete (ETC) tells you how much more budget is required to finish the project, given that everything continues at the current levels of performance. For more information, see Chapter 9 of Sybex's *PMP: Project Management Professional Study Guide*, 2nd Edition.

25. D. Checklists are a tool and technique of the Risk Identification process, not an information-gathering technique. For more information, see Chapter 6 of Sybex's *PMP: Project Management Professional Study Guide*, 2nd Edition.

26. C. Extrinsic motivators are material rewards like bonuses or stock options. Religious influences are an example of an intrinsic motivator. For more information, see Chapter 8 of Sybex's *PMP: Project Management Professional Study Guide*, 2nd Edition.

27. B. The Planning process has two inputs: Initiating and Controlling. The Executing process has two inputs: Planning and Controlling. The Controlling process input is the Executing process, and the Closing process input is the Controlling process. For more information, see Chapter 1 of Sybex's *PMP: Project Management Professional Study Guide*, 2nd Edition.

28. B. The formula for present value is $PV = FV \div (1 + i)^n$. Plugging in the information from the question, the formula becomes $\$8,000 \div (1 + .07)^3 = \$6,530$. For more information, see Chapter 3 of Sybex's *PMP: Project Management Professional Study Guide*, 2nd Edition.

29. A. Launching your own business with this newly found product would be unethical and also qualifies as an appearance of impropriety. The risk to your current organization is significant, so the correct step to take is to inform the project sponsor and stakeholders before making the decision to sign on this vendor. For more information, see Chapter 12 of Sybex's *PMP: Project Management Professional Study Guide*, 2nd Edition.

30. C. Duration compression shortens the project schedule without changing the project scope. Crashing doesn't always give you a good alternative and typically increases project costs. Fast tracking typically increases risk and causes rework. For more information, see Chapter 7 of Sybex's *PMP: Project Management Professional Study Guide*, 2nd Edition.

31. C. Configuration management, a tool and technique of Integrated Change Control, documents the physical characteristics of the product of the project and ensures that the description is accurate and complete. For more information, see Chapter 10 of Sybex's *PMP: Project Management Professional Study Guide*, 2nd Edition.

32. D. Knowledge areas are a collection of processes that share similar themes and, therefore, benefit from the expertise of specific knowledge and skills in each of these areas. They bring together processes that have characteristics in common and span all the life cycle processes. For example, Project Time Management is performed during the Planning and Controlling life cycle phases. For more information, see Chapter 2 of Sybex's *PMP: Project Management Professional Study Guide*, 2nd Edition.

33. D. NPV and IRR will generally bring you to the same accept/reject decision. For more information, see Chapter 3 of Sybex's *PMP: Project Management Professional Study Guide*, 2nd Edition.

34. C. The product description will be progressively elaborated throughout the Planning process, but it is an input to Scope Planning, not a tool and technique. For more information, see Chapter 4 of Sybex's *PMP: Project Management Professional Study Guide*, 2nd Edition.

35. B. This is a time and materials contract, because the engineers fees are fixed but the equipment and supplies charges will not be known until they're purchased. For more information, see Chapter 6 of Sybex's *PMP: Project Management Professional Study Guide*, 2nd Edition.

36. A. The resource pool description is an input to the Resource Planning process and requires knowledge of the types of resources needed for resource planning. In the early phases, as this question describes, the pool description can be high-level ("a small number of prototype testers"), while later on in the project, more specifics are detailed regarding the resources. Resource requirements describe the types of resources and the quantity of resources needed to fulfill each element of the work package level of the WBS. For more information, see Chapter 5 of Sybex's *PMP: Project Management Professional Study Guide*, 2nd Edition.

37. C. Risk Management Planning is the foundation process within the Risk Management knowledge area. According to *A Guide to the PMBOK*, it's important to complete this process so that the level, type, and visibility of risk management are proportionate to the risk and the project's importance to the company. For more information, see Chapter 6 of Sybex's *PMP: Project Management Professional Study Guide*, 2nd Edition.

38. C. The Project Scope Management knowledge area covers the Initiation, Planning, and Controlling life cycle phases. For more information, see Chapter 2 of Sybex's *PMP: Project Management Professional Study Guide*, 2nd Edition.

39. C. The EAC formula for this question is (AC + BAC) − EV. Plugging in the numbers from the question, you get (138 + 200) − 145 = 193. For more information, see Chapter 9 of Sybex's *PMP: Project Management Professional Study Guide*, 2nd Edition.

40. B. The Project Cost Management knowledge area technique used when evaluating various alternatives is called life cycle costing. This technique considers acquisition, operating, and disposal costs. For more information, see Chapter 2 of Sybex's *PMP: Project Management Professional Study Guide*, 2nd Edition.

41. B. Training does not necessarily need to be completed prior to assigning team members. Training can occur during the course of the project. For more information, see Chapter 8 of Sybex's *PMP: Project Management Professional Study Guide*, 2nd Edition.

42. A. Expected staff assignments are a constraint of the project. There are identified in the Organizational Planning process input called constraints. Expected staff assignments say the organization of the project team will likely be influenced by the skills, specialized knowledge, and competencies of the individual project team members who will serve on the team. For more information, see Chapter 5 of Sybex's *PMP: Project Management Professional Study Guide*, 2nd Edition.

43. D. The CP for the project is 335 days, but the CPM uses single duration estimates—not multiple duration estimates—to determine the early start and finish, and late start and finish dates. You know this question is referring to CPM because of the mention of "float." For more information, see Chapter 7 of Sybex's *PMP: Project Management Professional Study Guide*, 2nd Edition.

44. D. Retrieval systems are ways to store and share project information among project team members. Information distribution methods are ways of getting the information to the project team members and stakeholders. For more information, see Chapter 8 of Sybex's *PMP: Project Management Professional Study Guide*, 2nd Edition.

45. C. This statement does describe some goals but not adequately. Goals should be measurable, time bound, accurate, realistic, and tangible. There are no measures or time mentioned in this statement. Requirements describe the specifications of the goals and typically wouldn't be mixed into a goal statement. The goal statement should be clear and concise. For more information, see Chapter 2 of Sybex's *PMP: Project Management Professional Study Guide*, 2nd Edition.

46. D. The work breakdown structure (WBS) is an input to the Scope Change Control process but no other Change Control processes. Change requests are an input to four of the seven Change Control processes. For more information, see Chapter 10 of Sybex's *PMP: Project Management Professional Study Guide*, 2nd Edition.

47. A. Large, complex projects may have multiple scope statements. As the work of the project is decomposed and assigned, project teams may develop their own scope statements for a specific deliverable to describe the work needed to produce or complete the deliverable. For more information, see Chapter 4 of Sybex's *PMP: Project Management Professional Study Guide*, 2nd Edition.

**48.** D. Deliverables are measurable outcomes, measurable results, or specific items that must be produced to consider the project or project phase complete. Requirements are the specifications of the deliverables and tell you how you know the deliverable was completed successfully. For more information, see Chapter 2 of Sybex's *PMP: Project Management Professional Study Guide*, 2nd Edition.

**49.** C. Tracking includes a description of how you'll document the history of the risk activities for the current project and how the risk processes will be audited. This section of the risk management plan is also helpful for lessons learned. For more information, see Chapter 6 of Sybex's *PMP: Project Management Professional Study Guide*, 2nd Edition.

**50.** A. Assumptions are events or actions believed to be true. Answer B, C, and D are all constraints as they restrict or dictate the actions of the project team. For more information, see Chapter 2 of Sybex's *PMP: Project Management Professional Study Guide*, 2nd Edition.

**51.** A. The payback period for both of these alternatives is the same, so you cannot choose between them based on this information alone. The payback period for Alternative B is calculated as follows: Year 1 inflows = $36,000, Year 2 inflows = $36,000, for a total of $72,000 in 24 months. The first quarter of the next year inflows = $4,000, bringing the total to the initial investment of $76,000. The payback period is 27 months. For more information, see Chapter 3 of Sybex's *PMP: Project Management Professional Study Guide*, 2nd Edition.

**52.** B. The four steps of decomposition are: identify major deliverables, determine adequate cost and duration estimates, identify constituent components, and verify correctness of decomposition. No mention was made in the question of verifying the correctness of decomposition, so Answer A is not correct. The Detailed Planning deliverable has had the first three steps of the decomposition process performed. Answer D is not correct, because all the deliverables—with the exception of Detailed Planning—have had step one and two performed. For more information, see Chapter 4 of Sybex's *PMP: Project Management Professional Study Guide*, 2nd Edition.

**53.** D. There isn't enough information in this question to determine an answer. Payback period is the least precise of cash flow analysis techniques, but in this question, the payback periods are all the same. Initial investment isn't enough information to help choose among the projects. For more information, see Chapter 3 of Sybex's *PMP: Project Management Professional Study Guide*, 2nd Edition.

**54.** C. According to *A Guide to the PMBOK,* flowcharting can help the project team anticipate and identify where quality problems might occur on the project, which in turn, helps the team develop alternative approaches for dealing with the quality problems. For more information, see Chapter 6 of Sybex's *PMP: Project Management Professional Study Guide*, 2nd Edition.

**55.** A. The Risk Identification outputs are risks, triggers, and inputs to other processes. For more information, see Chapter 6 of Sybex's *PMP: Project Management Professional Study Guide*, 2nd Edition.

**56.** A. Cost, schedule, functionality, and quality risks, according to *A Guide to the PMBOK,* can be evaluated separately using their own independent ratings. For more information, see Chapter 6 of Sybex's *PMP: Project Management Professional Study Guide*, 2nd Edition.

**57.** A. Standard deviation is calculated as:

(Pessimistic − Optimistic) ÷ 6

The formula for this question is:

(24 − 18) ÷ 6 = 1

For more information, see Chapter 7 of Sybex's *PMP: Project Management Professional Study Guide*, 2nd Edition.

**58.** D. Schedule Development is not an input to Cost Budgeting, and Cost Budgeting is not in input to Schedule Development so these processes can be performed independently as long as both processes are completed prior to starting the Project Plan Development process. For more information, see Chapter 7 of Sybex's *PMP: Project Management Professional Study Guide*, 2nd Edition.

**59.** A. The purpose of the Team Development process is to create an open, encouraging environment for stakeholders to contribute and to develop your team into an effective, functioning, coordinated group. For more information, see Chapter 8 of Sybex's *PMP: Project Management Professional Study Guide*, 2nd Edition.

**60.** B. The Achievement Theory proposes the importance of friendship and a sense of camaraderie with other team members as a motivator. For more information, see Chapter 8 of Sybex's *PMP: Project Management Professional Study Guide*, 2nd Edition.

**61.** D. The Performance Reporting process involves collecting and distributing information regarding the performance of the project and is done using status reports, progress reports, and forecasting. For more information, see Chapter 9 of Sybex's *PMP: Project Management Professional Study Guide*, 2nd Edition.

**62.** D. The schedule variance (SV) and the schedule performance index (SPI) are two performance measurements that pertain to variances in schedule dates. For more information, see Chapter 10 of Sybex's *PMP: Project Management Professional Study Guide*, 2nd Edition.

**63.** A. Lessons learned is not a process—it's an output of several processes. For more information, see Chapter 11 of Sybex's *PMP: Project Management Professional Study Guide*, 2nd Edition.

**64.** D. The Scope Definition process, according to *A Guide to the PMOBK*, on page 57, is critical to project success, improves the accuracy of estimates, defines a baseline for measurement and control, and facilitates responsibility assignments. Decomposition breaks deliverables down into smaller components, not deliverables as option D states. For more information, see Chapter 4 of Sybex's *PMP: Project Management Professional Study Guide*, 2nd Edition.

# Answers to Final Exam Review 3

1. **D.** Culture shock occurs when a person is working in an unfamiliar environment and their experiences and the actions of others around them are not as they expect. For more information, see Chapter 12 of Sybex's *PMP: Project Management Professional Study Guide*, 2nd Edition.

2. **B.** The EAC formula for this question is AC + ((BAC − EV) ÷ CPI). CPI = EV ÷ AC. First, calculate CPI: 145 ÷ 138 = 1.05. Plugging in the numbers from the question, you get 138 + ((200 − 145) ÷ 1.05) = 190.4. For more information, see Chapter 9 of Sybex's *PMP: Project Management Professional Study Guide*, 2nd Edition.

3. **D.** The communications management plan (an output of the Communications Planning process) is implemented during the Information Distribution process. For more information, see Chapter 8 of Sybex's *PMP: Project Management Professional Study Guide*, 2nd Edition.

4. **B.** The identification and classification of scope changes is documented in the scope management plan, which is part of the Scope Planning process, not the Scope Definition process. For more information, see Chapter 4 of Sybex's *PMP: Project Management Professional Study Guide*, 2nd Edition.

5. **C.** The resource calendar reflects the periods of work that specific resources—or groups of resources—are available to work on the project. Resource calendars are an input to the Schedule Development process. For more information, see Chapter 7 of Sybex's *PMP: Project Management Professional Study Guide*, 2nd Edition.

6. **C.** When a project is performed under contract, pricing determines how much the organization will charge for producing the product or service of the project. For more information, see Chapter 5 of Sybex's *PMP: Project Management Professional Study Guide*, 2nd Edition.

7. **B.** As a PMP, one of your responsibilities is to support the *PMP Code of Professional Conduct* and make certain others have copies or access to it. As the project manager, you should require all PMPs on the project to have a copy and read it. For more information, see Chapter 12 of Sybex's *PMP: Project Management Professional Study Guide*, 2nd Edition.

8. **B.** Qualitative Risk Analysis determines the probability and impact of risks on the project objectives, ranks risks in priority order, and assigns an overall risk ranking for the project. For more information, see Chapter 6 of Sybex's *PMP: Project Management Professional Study Guide*, 2nd Edition.

9. **D.** The scope statement and the WBS are inputs to both the Resource Planning and the Activity Definition process. However, Activity Definition should not be part of this answer, since it focuses on Resource Planning process elements. Resources are determined, quantities of resources have been identified, and the timing of the resources needed to perform the activities has been determined. The question describes linking the resources with the activities. The activities have already been decomposed from the WBS resulting in the activity list, which is an output of the Activity Definition process. For more information, see Chapter 5 of Sybex's *PMP: Project Management Professional Study Guide*, 2nd Edition.

10. A. Leadership, communication, and negotiation skills are the three most important general knowledge skills needed during Project Plan Execution. All general management skills are needed during this process, but these are essential. For more information, see Chapter 8 of Sybex's *PMP: Project Management Professional Study Guide*, 2nd Edition.

11. D. The formula for future value is $FV = PV(1 + i)^n$. Plugging in the information from the question, the formula becomes $\$10,000 (1 + .05)^2 = \$11,025$. For more information, see Chapter 3 of Sybex's *PMP: Project Management Professional Study Guide*, 2nd Edition.

12. C. Change requests are an output of the Project Plan Execution process and are an input to the Cost Control and Integrated Change Control processes. For more information, see Chapter 8 of Sybex's *PMP: Project Management Professional Study Guide*, 2nd Edition.

13. B. Product analysis is a tool and technique of Scope Planning, and according to *A Guide to the PMBOK*, uses techniques such as product breakdown analysis, systems engineering, value engineering, value analysis, function analysis, and quality function deployment. For more information, see Chapter 4 of Sybex's *PMP: Project Management Professional Study Guide*, 2nd Edition.

14. A. Control charts can be used to monitor any type of output variable—including project management processes—but are most often used to track repetitive activities. For more information, see Chapter 10 of Sybex's *PMP: Project Management Professional Study Guide*, 2nd Edition.

15. D. Progressive elaboration is a process of defining the characteristics of the product or service of the project incrementally into further and further detail. For more information, see Chapter 1 of Sybex's *PMP: Project Management Professional Study Guide*, 2nd Edition.

16. D. The tools and techniques of the Organizational Planning process are templates, human resource practices, organizational theory, and stakeholder analysis. For more information, see Chapter 5 of Sybex's *PMP: Project Management Professional Study Guide*, 2nd Edition.

17. B. According to *A Guide to the PMBOK*, page 140, "The effectiveness of response planning will directly determine whether risk increases or decreases for the project." For more information, see Chapter 6 of Sybex's *PMP: Project Management Professional Study Guide*, 2nd Edition.

18. D. Indexed records are project records created during the Administrative Closure process, but this question is referring to the Contract Closeout process. That means Answer D is the least correct answer. For more information, see Chapter 12 of Sybex's *PMP: Project Management Professional Study Guide*, 2nd Edition.

19. B. This question describes a series of phases used to publish a book. Phase sequencing involves a series of handoffs from one phase to the next. In this question, the project manager is required to obtain approval on one phase before handoff can occur to the next phase. For more information, see Chapter 1 of Sybex's *PMP: Project Management Professional Study Guide*, 2nd Edition.

20. C. Rebaselining typically occurs as a result of cost or schedule revisions (which can be caused by scope changes). Quality Control is concerned with product results and project management results such as cost and schedule performance. Quality Control is also concerned with eliminating unsatisfactory results. For more information, see Chapter 10 of Sybex's *PMP: Project Management Professional Study Guide*, 2nd Edition.

21. A. A change to the agreed-upon WBS tells you we're talking about scope changes. Scope changes are managed with the scope change control system (a tool and technique of this process), which this question also mentions. The scope change was approved and appropriate planning processes already were updated, as the question states. While answers B, C, and D may seem correct, the question states that the project costs and project schedule have changed due to the approved change. Costs and schedules are baselines that might be significantly impacted when changes to scope occur. This question states that the changes are substantial, so the baselines should be adjusted. Adjusted baseline is an output of the Scope Change Control process. For more information, see Chapter 10 of Sybex's *PMP: Project Management Professional Study Guide*, 2nd Edition.

22. D. The payback period is the least precise of all the cash flow techniques, not discounted cash flow. For more information, see Chapter 3 of Sybex's *PMP: Project Management Professional Study Guide*, 2nd Edition.

23. D. Screening systems use predetermined performance criteria or minimum requirements of performance to rate vendors. For more information, see Chapter 9 of Sybex's *PMP: Project Management Professional Study Guide*, 2nd Edition.

24. D. Estimate at completion (EAC) is the expected cost of the work when completed. For more information, see Chapter 9 of Sybex's *PMP: Project Management Professional Study Guide*, 2nd Edition.

25. D. This question describes a balanced matrix organization. The title of the position is project manager, which tells you it's either a balanced or strong matrix organization. The fact that Jim the team member has a functional manager who is your peer tells you that this organization is a balanced matrix. For more information, see Chapter 1 of Sybex's *PMP: Project Management Professional Study Guide*, 2nd Edition.

26. B. GERT takes into account probabilistic treatment of the activity duration estimates. Some activities may only be performed in part, some more than once, and others not at all. For more information, see Chapter 7 of Sybex's *PMP: Project Management Professional Study Guide*, 2nd Edition.

27. C. The project manager's primary responsibilities include planning, executing, and managing the project according to the project plan. The project manager may not even be identified until the close of the Initiation process or phase. For more information, see Chapter 3 of Sybex's *PMP: Project Management Professional Study Guide*, 2nd Edition.

28. A. The Project Plan Execution, Performance Reporting, Quality Control, and Change Control project management processes must be applied during the Contract Administration process in order to manage contractual relationships and integrate the outputs of these processes within Contract Administration. For more information, see Chapter 9 of Sybex's *PMP: Project Management Professional Study Guide*, 2nd Edition.

29. B. General management skills are very likely to affect project outcomes. Cost Budgeting is part of the Planning process group, and Cost Control is part of the Controlling process group. PMI requires either a degree or a certain number of years of experience in project management to sit for the exam, along with other requirements. For more information, see Chapter 1 of Sybex's *PMP: Project Management Professional Study Guide*, 2nd Edition.

30. D. Recruitment practices are organizational procedures or policies that deal with hiring and assigning staff. For more information, see Chapter 5 of Sybex's *PMP: Project Management Professional Study Guide*, 2nd Edition.

31. B. The Activity Sequencing process produces network diagrams and updates to the activity list. The purpose of this process is to identify all activity dependencies. For more information, see Chapter 5 of Sybex's *PMP: Project Management Professional Study Guide*, 2nd Edition.

32. D. The outputs of the Scope Planning process are the scope statement, supporting detail, and the scope management plan. For more information, see Chapter 4 of Sybex's *PMP: Project Management Professional Study Guide*, 2nd Edition.

33. C. It's important for project managers to understand the organizational culture they're working in. Entrepreneurial, leading edge, aggressive organizations are likely to approve high-risk projects, and project managers are typically comfortable proposing new ideas and projects in this type of environment. For more information, see Chapter 1 of Sybex's *PMP: Project Management Professional Study Guide*, 2nd Edition.

34. C. When obtaining services from within the organization, the only process you'll perform is the Procurement Planning process. For more information, see Chapter 6 of Sybex's *PMP: Project Management Professional Study Guide*, 2nd Edition.

35. C. The inputs of the Communication Planning process are communications requirements, communications technology, assumptions, and constraints. For more information, see Chapter 4 of Sybex's *PMP: Project Management Professional Study Guide*, 2nd Edition.

36. C. This question describes Project Integration Management. The three processes in this knowledge area are Project Plan Development, Project Plan Execution, and Integrated Change Control. The question tells you the project plan is being executed (Project Plan Execution) and the customer has requested changes (Integrated Change Control). It also tells you that changes to the project plan are required (Project Plan Development) and the processes in this knowledge area are highly interactive. For more information, see Chapter 2 of Sybex's *PMP: Project Management Professional Study Guide*, 2nd Edition.

37. C. Payback period is the least precise of all cash flow calculations, so you shouldn't give this a lot of consideration if NPV is positive and IRR is greater than 0. Since Project B and Project D both have negative NPV, they shouldn't be chosen. Project C has a higher IRR value than Project A and should be the project you choose, even though its payback period is longer than project A. For more information, see Chapter 3 of Sybex's *PMP: Project Management Professional Study Guide*, 2nd Edition.

38. A. Risk categories are an input to the Risk Identification process. For more information, see Chapter 6 of Sybex's *PMP: Project Management Professional Study Guide*, 2nd Edition.

39. B. Monte Carlo analysis is the most commonly used simulation technique in the Schedule Development process. For more information, see Chapter 7 of Sybex's *PMP: Project Management Professional Study Guide*, 2nd Edition.

40. **B.** Project Scope Management is concerned with product scope and project scope. Product scope is concerned with the characteristics of the product or service of the project and is measured against the project requirements. Project scope is concerned with the work of the project and is measured against the project plan. For more information, see Chapter 2 of Sybex's *PMP: Project Management Professional Study Guide*, 2nd Edition.

41. **C.** As the project progresses through the life cycle, you should use different techniques to perform these processes, including using different techniques to motivate, lead, and coach. The techniques you'll use will depend on the makeup of the project team and the stakeholders involved in that stage. For more information, see Chapter 2 of Sybex's *PMP: Project Management Professional Study Guide*, 2nd Edition.

42. **D.** The WBS details the entire scope of the project and includes all deliverables. It is an output of the Scope Definition process. For more information, see Chapter 4 of Sybex's *PMP: Project Management Professional Study Guide*, 2nd Edition.

43. **C.** IRR is the discount rate when the present value of the cash inflows equals the original investment. Project A's original investment equals the present value of its cash inflows at a discount rate of eight percent. Therefore, Project A has the highest IRR and should be chosen above the other two. For more information, see Chapter 3 of Sybex's *PMP: Project Management Professional Study Guide*, 2nd Edition.

44. **D.** In practice, a procurement audit would reveal this information but according to *A Guide to the PMBOK*, procurement audits are performed from Procurement Planning through Contract Administration. This question describes the Contract Closeout process, because formal acceptance and closure are an output of Contract Closeout. Therefore, none of these answers are correct. For more information, see Chapter 11 of Sybex's *PMP: Project Management Professional Study Guide*, 2nd Edition.

45. **A.** This came about due to a business need. Staff members were spending unproductive hours converting information, causing the company loss. The time the employees spent converting the information could have been spent doing something more productive. For more information, see Chapter 2 of Sybex's *PMP: Project Management Professional Study Guide*, 2nd Edition.

46. **D.** Qualitative Risk Analysis involves determining what impact the identified risks will have on the project and the probability they'll occur. Quantitative Risk Analysis looks at the risks you've identified and assigns numeric probabilities to each risk and their impacts. Quantitative Risk Analysis evaluates the impacts of risk and quantifies the risk exposure of the project. It determines any interactions among the risks and assesses the range of potential project outcomes. The tools and techniques of the Quantitative Risk Analysis process are interviewing, sensitivity analysis, decision tree analysis, and simulation. For more information, see Chapter 6 of Sybex's *PMP: Project Management Professional Study Guide*, 2nd Edition.

47. **B.** This is a constraint, because the actions of the project team are restricted due to the hardware policy. For more information, see Chapter 2 of Sybex's *PMP: Project Management Professional Study Guide*, 2nd Edition.

**48.** D. An assumption is an event or action believed to be true. Two assumptions are stated in this question. You assume that the person who worked the equipment deliverable on the last project of this nature will be assigned to your project and that he understands the newest equipment updates and needs. For more information, see Chapter 2 of Sybex's *PMP: Project Management Professional Study Guide*, 2nd Edition.

**49.** C. The six needs or demands are market demand, business need, customer request, technological advance, legal requirement, and social need. For more information, see Chapter 2 of Sybex's *PMP: Project Management Professional Study Guide*, 2nd Edition.

**50.** D. The arrow diagramming method sometimes requires the use of dummy activities in order to define the logical relationships correctly. For more information, see Chapter 5 of Sybex's *PMP: Project Management Professional Study Guide*, 2nd Edition.

**51.** D. Quality Planning has four outputs: quality management plan, operational definitions, checklists, and inputs to other processes. Benchmarking is a tool and technique of this process. For more information, see Chapter 6 of Sybex's *PMP: Project Management Professional Study Guide*, 2nd Edition.

**52.** B. The Delphi technique reduces bias in the data. The nominal group technique is similar to the Delphi technique, but *A Guide to the PMBOK* states that Delphi reduces bias. For more information, see Chapter 6 of Sybex's *PMP: Project Management Professional Study Guide*, 2nd Edition.

**53.** B. This is an example of a linear cardinal scale. Risk scales reflect the severity of the effects of the risk consequences to the project objectives. For more information, see Chapter 6 of Sybex's *PMP: Project Management Professional Study Guide*, 2nd Edition.

**54.** B. The expected value is calculated as:

(Optimistic + Pessimistic + (4 × Most Likely)) ÷ 6

The formula for this question is:

(18 + 22 + (4 × 20)) ÷ 6 = 20

CPM uses the most likely estimate to determine activity duration estimates, which is 20. For more information, see Chapter 7 of Sybex's *PMP: Project Management Professional Study Guide*, 2nd Edition.

**55.** A. According to *A Guide to the PMBOK*, the project plan changes as the project progresses and more information is known. Performance measurement baselines typically only change when the project scope or project deliverables change and those changes are approved. For more information, see Chapter 7 of Sybex's *PMP: Project Management Professional Study Guide*, 2nd Edition.

**56.** C. This confrontation describes the storming stage of team development. For more information, see Chapter 8 of Sybex's *PMP: Project Management Professional Study Guide*, 2nd Edition.

**57.** D. The best answer to this question is D. Theory X managers believe people are motivated only by punishment, money, or position. This manager has made a point of telling you about her position and threatened you with punishment if you don't shape up. For more information, see Chapter 8 of Sybex's *PMP: Project Management Professional Study Guide*, 2nd Edition.

**58.** D. Earned value analysis integrates scope, cost, and schedule measures to analyze project performance. It is the most commonly used method of performance measurement. For more information, see Chapter 9 of Sybex's *PMP: Project Management Professional Study Guide*, 2nd Edition.

**59.** D. Other terms for change control board include technical assessment board (TAB), technical review board (TRB), engineering review board (ERB), and change control board (CCB). For more information, see Chapter 10 of Sybex's *PMP: Project Management Professional Study Guide*, 2nd Edition.

**60.** D. Change requests are an input to the Integrated Change Control process, and product skills and knowledge are a tool and technique of the Project Plan Execution process. For more information, see Chapter 4 of Sybex's *PMP: Project Management Professional Study Guide*, 2nd Edition.

**61.** C. Changes to the start and finish dates of activities in the schedule are called revisions. When changes are made to the schedule that will cause significant schedule delays, you should rebaseline the schedule. For more information, see Chapter 10 of Sybex's *PMP: Project Management Professional Study Guide*, 2nd Edition.

**62.** C. The Scope Verification process is where the level of detail concerning the amount of work completed is documented. For more information, see Chapter 11 of Sybex's *PMP: Project Management Professional Study Guide*, 2nd Edition.

**63.** C. The best answer in this situation is to get the facts before taking any action. A violation based on rumors only should not be reported. You can get the facts by telling your friend you're concerned about the appearance of impropriety and ask her if the vendor gave her these items. It could be that these are the first of several samples that will be coming from all the vendors bidding on the project so the equipment can be evaluated in light of the project objectives. Or, she could have accepted them as gifts, which is not appropriate. Never jump to conclusions. Always ask and get the facts straight before reporting a conflict of interest situation. For more information, see Chapter 12 of Sybex's *PMP: Project Management Professional Study Guide*, 2nd Edition.

**64.** C. This question describes the Scope Planning process because you're progressively elaborating the work of the project. The project charter has been published (this is one input to this process), and you've reviewed the product description (another input to this process). The tools and techniques described in this question are alternatives identification and expert judgment. Your interview of the two key stakeholders is expert judgment, and their alternative suggestions are considered alternatives identification. For more information, see Chapter 4 of Sybex's *PMP: Project Management Professional Study Guide*, 2nd Edition.

# Answers to Final Exam Review 4

1. **C.** A project has a definite starting and ending date, is temporary, and exists to create a unique product or service. Each conference is unique, with a definite starting and ending date. The preparations required to design and prepare the vendor booth are specific to the conference; therefore this is a project. Answer A is not correct because Closing processes should always be conducted, even when projects are canceled. Answer D is not correct because there is not enough information in the question to determine if these processes were completed. The processes within the Project Integration Management knowledge area are Project Plan Development, Project Plan Execution, and Integrated Change Control. For more information, see Chapter 1 of Sybex's *PMP: Project Management Professional Study Guide*, 2nd Edition.

2. **C.** The appropriate action on your part is to instruct this person not to wear this piece of jewelry to work. Others find it offensive—as they've told you—and it's not appropriate for the work environment you're working in. For more information, see Chapter 12 of Sybex's *PMP: Project Management Professional Study Guide*, 2nd Edition.

3. **C.** Legitimate power comes about as a result of the position the person holds who's doing the influencing. In this case, you're the project manager and have legitimate power to execute the work of this deliverable the way you see fit. For more information, see Chapter 8 of Sybex's *PMP: Project Management Professional Study Guide*, 2nd Edition.

4. **B.** Risks are uncertain events that may be threats or opportunities to the objectives of the project. For more information, see Chapter 6 of Sybex's *PMP: Project Management Professional Study Guide*, 2nd Edition.

5. **B.** The best answer for the question is option B because Resource Planning involves identifying the physical resources needed for the project. The question states that a robotics expert (a resource) is needed for two phases of the project. The Cost Estimating process determines an approximate cost of the resource. For more information, see Chapter 5 of Sybex's *PMP: Project Management Professional Study Guide*, 2nd Edition.

6. **A.** The scope management plan describes how scope changes will be managed and incorporated into the project. It also describes how scope changes will be identified and classified. The scope management plan should also address the likelihood of scope changes, how often they might occur, and how much. Changes to cost are addressed in the cost management plan, changes to quality are addressed in the quality management plan, and changes to schedule are addressed in the schedule management plan. For more information, see Chapter 4 of Sybex's *PMP: Project Management Professional Study Guide*, 2nd Edition.

7. **D.** Trend analysis is a tool and technique of Quality Control and Performance Reporting. It's a mathematical formula used to forecast future outcomes. For more information, see Chapter 10 of Sybex's *PMP: Project Management Professional Study Guide*, 2nd Edition.

**8.** B. The project champion, unlike the project sponsor, is not necessarily an executive, nor do they have the authority to make decisions. They are often called upon to contribute to decisions, but the project sponsor has the final authority on project decisions and issues. For more information, see Chapter 3 of Sybex's *PMP: Project Management Professional Study Guide*, 2nd Edition.

**9.** D. The reward is in line with the performance, but the functional manager is the one who should receive this reward since they're the one who kept costs in line with the budget. For more information, see Chapter 8 of Sybex's *PMP: Project Management Professional Study Guide*, 2nd Edition.

**10.** C. Phase sequencing is still being followed, even though you're using a fast tracking technique to compress the time. You can deduce that time is a constraint on this project, because the project sponsor is concerned about finishing on schedule. The project schedule is being compressed by overlapping phases. For more information, see Chapter 1 of Sybex's *PMP: Project Management Professional Study Guide*, 2nd Edition.

**11.** A. The project calendar affects all the resources of the project and reflects the periods of time the work will be performed in. Resource calendars affect specific resources—or groups of resources—and show things like vacation or training time. Calendars are an input to the Schedule Development process. For more information, see Chapter 7 of Sybex's *PMP: Project Management Professional Study Guide*, 2nd Edition.

**12.** D. Performance measurement documentation contains the records that analyze and detail project performance. For more information, see Chapter 11 of Sybex's *PMP: Project Management Professional Study Guide*, 2nd Edition.

**13.** D. There isn't enough information in the question to determine if there is a lack of product knowledge on Mishi's part. Product knowledge pertains to the product of the project, and this question addresses a corrective action needed regarding an accounting issue, which is a general management skill. For more information, see Chapter 8 of Sybex's *PMP: Project Management Professional Study Guide*, 2nd Edition.

**14.** C. The project manager's role and responsibility, according to the Organizational Planning process, is generally critical for most projects. For more information, see Chapter 5 of Sybex's *PMP: Project Management Professional Study Guide*, 2nd Edition.

**15.** C. Evaluation criteria are an output of Solicitation Planning and an input of Source Selection. The criteria may be either objective or subjective. For more information, see Chapter 9 of Sybex's *PMP: Project Management Professional Study Guide*, 2nd Edition.

**16.** A. Composite organizations are a combination of all organizational types and typically involve a projectized structure coexisting within a functional organization. For more information, see Chapter 1 of Sybex's *PMP: Project Management Professional Study Guide*, 2nd Edition.

**17.** A. Product skills and knowledge are a tool and technique of the Project Plan Execution process. For more information, see Chapter 8 of Sybex's *PMP: Project Management Professional Study Guide*, 2nd Edition.

18. C. This is a finish-to-start (FS) relationship. The start of the work of the painter depends on the completion of the work of the gutter crew. ADM diagrams use only the finish-to-start (FS) relationship. PDM diagrams may use four types of precedence relationships. For more information, see Chapter 5 of Sybex's *PMP: Project Management Professional Study Guide*, 2nd Edition.

19. D. This is an example of a force majeure risk, which is external to the project. Force majeure risks are included in the external risk category, which is a subset of the risk categories input of the Risk Identification process. For more information, see Chapter 6 of Sybex's *PMP: Project Management Professional Study Guide*, 2nd Edition.

20. C. Qualified sellers lists are a list of vendors that have been prequalified to provide contract services or provide supplies and materials to the organization. This is an input to the Solicitation process, which is concerned with obtaining responses to RFPs from vendors. For more information, see Chapter 9 of Sybex's *PMP: Project Management Professional Study Guide*, 2nd Edition.

21. C. Schedule variance tells you if the schedule is ahead or behind what was planned for this period and is calculated by subtracting PV from EV. In this case, the formula looks like this: $95 - 85 = 10$. The resulting number is positive, which means the schedule is ahead of what was planned for this time period. For more information, see Chapter 9 of Sybex's *PMP: Project Management Professional Study Guide*, 2nd Edition.

22. C. This project ended due to starvation, because the grant money was not renewed. For more information, see Chapter 11 of Sybex's *PMP: Project Management Professional Study Guide*, 2nd Edition.

23. C. The Cost Budgeting process produces the cost baseline for the project, which is a time-phased budget used throughout the project. Cost Budgeting is a core process that must be completed prior to the completion of the Project Plan Development process of which the project plan is an output. For more information, see Chapter 7 of Sybex's *PMP: Project Management Professional Study Guide*, 2nd Edition.

24. B. Problem solving involves asking questions to separate the causes of the problem from the symptoms. Decision making involves considering alternative solutions to the problem. Choices are made from among the alternatives. Timing is important in decision making, because good decisions made too soon or too late can turn into inferior solutions. For more information, see Chapter 1 of Sybex's *PMP: Project Management Professional Study Guide*, 2nd Edition.

25. D. The project team must consider the characteristics of potential team members, whether they're from inside or outside the organization. This question describes staffing pool descriptions, which are an input to Staff Acquisition. For more information, see Chapter 5 of Sybex's *PMP: Project Management Professional Study Guide*, 2nd Edition.

26. A. While each of these items may also require influencing, problem-solving, and communication skills, these items are specifically listed as typical negotiation topics in *A Guide to the PMBOK*. For more information, see Chapter 1 of Sybex's *PMP: Project Management Professional Study Guide*, 2nd Edition.

27. D. A purchase order, memorandum of understanding, agreement, and subcontract are all terms for contract according to *A Guide to the PMBOK*. For more information, see Chapter 9 of Sybex's *PMP: Project Management Professional Study Guide*, 2nd Edition.

28. A. A positive value for NPV means the project will earn a return at least equal to or greater than the cost of capital. Since NPV for Alternative A is positive, this alternative will earn at least a 12 percent return. For more information, see Chapter 3 of Sybex's *PMP: Project Management Professional Study Guide*, 2nd Edition.

29. C. Procurement audits review the procurement process from Procurement Planning through Contract Administration. The RFP process is part of the Solicitation Planning process, which would be reviewed as part of a procurement audit. For more information, see Chapter 11 of Sybex's *PMP: Project Management Professional Study Guide*, 2nd Edition.

30. A. PERT uses expected value (the weighted average of three time estimates) to determine activity start and finish dates. CPM uses one time estimate—the most likely—to determine start and finish dates. For more information, see Chapter 7 of Sybex's *PMP: Project Management Professional Study Guide*, 2nd Edition.

31. A. Earned Value Management (EVM) is an integrating methodology that helps integrate the project processes and measure project performance. For more information, see Chapter 2 of Sybex's *PMP: Project Management Professional Study Guide*, 2nd Edition.

32. A. First, you need to know EAC. The EAC formula for this question is AC + ETC. Plugging in the numbers from the question, you get 138 + 62 = 200. VAC = BAC − EAC. Therefore, 200 − 200 = 0. For more information, see Chapter 9 of Sybex's *PMP: Project Management Professional Study Guide*, 2nd Edition.

33. D. Carrie used the analogous estimating technique, which is a form of expert judgment. It is a tool and technique of the Activity Duration Estimating process. Analogous estimating bases estimates on previous activities that are similar in fact, and they require the person estimating them to have expertise with the activity. Analogous estimating techniques are typically used to estimate project duration when there is a limited amount of information about the project. For more information, see Chapter 5 of Sybex's *PMP: Project Management Professional Study Guide*, 2nd Edition.

34. A. The best answer to this question is A. The project status input to the Qualitative Risk Analysis process refers to examining the life cycle phase the project is currently in and realizing that as the project progresses, changes will occur and new risks may come to light or previously identified risks may take on new consequences. Qualitative Risk Analysis should be performed throughout the life of the project. Note that Quantitative Risk Analysis may not be required for a project, as detailed by the project team in the risk management plan. For more information, see Chapter 6 of Sybex's *PMP: Project Management Professional Study Guide*, 2nd Edition.

**35.** C. Project Integration Management uses two techniques: Earned Value Management (EVM) and project management software. For more information, see Chapter 2 of Sybex's *PMP: Project Management Professional Study Guide*, 2nd Edition.

**36.** C. Scope change control is a system that tracks and records change requests, describes the procedures to follow to implement scope change, and details the authorization levels needed to approve the changes. When a project is performed under contract, scope changes must conform to the provisions of the contract. For more information, see Chapter 10 of Sybex's *PMP: Project Management Professional Study Guide*, 2nd Edition.

**37.** A. This question requires discounted cash flow analysis to compare the value of Alternative A to Alternative B. Applying the present value formula to Alternative A is calculated this way: $\$98,000 \div (1 + .08)^2 = \$84,019$. Alternative B is calculated this way: $\$105,000 \div (1 + .08)^3 = \$83,352$. For more information, see Chapter 3 of Sybex's *PMP: Project Management Professional Study Guide*, 2nd Edition.

**38.** B. Project Communications Management involves every member of the project team, including all the stakeholders. Everyone involved on the project will send or receive project information or do both. Project Human Resources involves all the human resources assigned to the work of the project. While all the folks working on the project are involved, only the project manager and perhaps a few others are involved in performing the processes within this knowledge area. For more information, see Chapter 2 of Sybex's *PMP: Project Management Professional Study Guide*, 2nd Edition.

**39.** D. Transference is the most effective response in dealing with financial risks. This almost always involves paying a premium for the transfer of risk. For more information, see Chapter 6 of Sybex's *PMP: Project Management Professional Study Guide*, 2nd Edition.

**40.** C. Projects with large budgets may or may not be managed by the project manager. There are no rules or guidelines that state that projects with large project expense budgets be managed by a functional manager. For more information, see Chapter 3 of Sybex's *PMP: Project Management Professional Study Guide*, 2nd Edition.

**41.** B. According to *A Guide to the PMBOK*, page 58, "The major deliverables should always be defined in terms of how the project will actually be organized." In this question, the project is organized according to phases, so decomposition should follow this structure. For more information, see Chapter 4 of Sybex's *PMP: Project Management Professional Study Guide*, 2nd Edition.

**42.** D. The purpose of a project overview is to capture the intended project outcomes and identify the project deliverables. A detailed project schedule is not part of the project overview. However, you might include some key milestones in the project overview if they're known. For more information, see Chapter 2 of Sybex's *PMP: Project Management Professional Study Guide*, 2nd Edition.

**43.** C. Management directives are constraints, because they either restrict or dictate the actions of the project team. For more information, see Chapter 2 of Sybex's *PMP: Project Management Professional Study Guide*, 2nd Edition.

**44.** B. When risks have high impacts or the strategy identified to deal with this risk is not fully effective, a fallback plan should be developed. For more information, see Chapter 6 of Sybex's *PMP: Project Management Professional Study Guide*, 2nd Edition.

**45.** A. Assumptions are events or actions believed to be true. Answer B, C, and D are all constraints, because they restrict or dictate the actions of the project team. For more information, see Chapter 2 of Sybex's *PMP: Project Management Professional Study Guide*, 2nd Edition.

**46.** B. IRR is the discount rate when the present value of the cash inflows equals the original investment. Projects with the highest IRR value should be selected so Alternative A is the best option. For more information, see Chapter 3 of Sybex's *PMP: Project Management Professional Study Guide*, 2nd Edition.

**47.** A. Analogous—or top-down—estimating techniques are a form of expert judgment. Since this project is similar to another recent project, you can use the cost estimates from the previous project to help you quickly determine estimates for the current project. For more information, see Chapter 5 of Sybex's *PMP: Project Management Professional Study Guide*, 2nd Edition.

**48.** B. Parametric modeling uses variables—or parameters—to produce cost estimates. Contingencies are also known as reserve time and are used in the Activity Duration Estimating process. For more information, see Chapter 5 of Sybex's *PMP: Project Management Professional Study Guide*, 2nd Edition.

**49.** D. The outputs of the Activity Duration Estimating process are activity duration estimates, basis of estimates, and activity list updates. Activity duration estimates must always include a range of possible results. For example, Hugh's activity should be recorded as 30 days ± 5 days, not simply 30 days as he gave you. The documented assumptions are a result of the basis of estimates output, and the activity list is updated as a result of this process, not the WBS, according to the *A Guide to the PMBOK*. For more information, see Chapter 5 of Sybex's *PMP: Project Management Professional Study Guide*, 2nd Edition.

**50.** A. Data precision ranking is a tool and technique of the Qualitative Risk Analysis process. The remaining tool and technique of Quantitative Risk Analysis is simulation. For more information, see Chapter 6 of Sybex's *PMP: Project Management Professional Study Guide*, 2nd Edition.

**51.** B. Organizational risks typically include time, cost, scope objectives that are inconsistent, a lack of funding, a lack of prioritization or changing priorities, and resource conflicts with other projects the organization has undertaken. For more information, see Chapter 6 of Sybex's *PMP: Project Management Professional Study Guide*, 2nd Edition.

**52.** B. First, you need to know EAC. The EAC formula for this question is (AC + BAC) – EV. Plugging in the numbers from the question, you get (138 + 200) – 145 = 193. ETC = EAC – AC. Therefore, 193 – 138 = 55. For more information, see Chapter 9 of Sybex's *PMP: Project Management Professional Study Guide*, 2nd Edition.

**53.** D. Assessing risk probability is difficult because it relies on expert judgment. For more information, see Chapter 6 of Sybex's *PMP: Project Management Professional Study Guide*, 2nd Edition.

**54.** C. The duration of Path A is 19, the duration of Path B is 22, the duration of Path C is 21, and the duration of Path D is 21. Therefore, Path B (answer C) is the critical path since it's the longest path on the project. For more information, see Chapter 7 of Sybex's *PMP: Project Management Professional Study Guide*, 2nd Edition.

**55.** D. Benefit/cost analysis is a technique used to consider the costs and benefits of various project or product alternatives. It includes techniques such as return on investment and payback period. For more information, see Chapter 4 of Sybex's *PMP: Project Management Professional Study Guide*, 2nd Edition.

**56.** C. Planning outputs are an input to the Project Plan Development process and make sure to consider all of the outputs of the Planning processes, not just the core Planning processes. For more information, see Chapter 7 of Sybex's *PMP: Project Management Professional Study Guide*, 2nd Edition.

**57.** A. Whenever a new team member is introduced, the team development stages start over with the forming stage. For more information, see Chapter 8 of Sybex's *PMP: Project Management Professional Study Guide*, 2nd Edition.

**58.** B. You've been threatened with consequences if your behavior doesn't change, which is an example of punishment power. For more information, see Chapter 8 of Sybex's *PMP: Project Management Professional Study Guide*, 2nd Edition.

**59.** B. Cost variance tells you if costs are higher or lower than budgeted and is calculated by subtracting AC from EV. In this case, the formula looks like this: 85 − 100 = <15>. Negative numbers mean the costs are higher than budgeted. For more information, see Chapter 9 of Sybex's *PMP: Project Management Professional Study Guide*, 2nd Edition.

**60.** B. Variance analysis is the key tool and technique for controlling project time. For more information, see Chapter 10 of Sybex's *PMP: Project Management Professional Study Guide*, 2nd Edition.

**61.** B. Inspection is about keeping mistakes in the product from getting to the customers. Testing prior to delivering the product to your customer is an example of this. For more information, see Chapter 10 of Sybex's *PMP: Project Management Professional Study Guide*, 2nd Edition.

**62.** D. Administrative Closure ensures that project records accurately reflect the final specifications of the product. It also analyzes project management processes for effectiveness, and roles and responsibilities documentation should be updated during this process. Verifying and accepting the product documentation is performed during the Scope Verification process. For more information, see Chapter 11 of Sybex's *PMP: Project Management Professional Study Guide*, 2nd Edition.

63. B. Documenting the requirements, performing inspections, and requesting acceptance and sign-off at important milestones are all acceptable ways to ensure customer satisfaction. For more information, see Chapter 12 of Sybex's *PMP: Project Management Professional Study Guide*, 2nd Edition.

64. B. According to *A Guide to the PMBOK*, pg. 55, "Scope Planning is the process of progressively elaborating and documenting the project work (project scope) that produces the product of the project." For more information, see Chapter 4 of Sybex's *PMP: Project Management Professional Study Guide*, 2nd Edition.

# Project Management Skills for all Levels

### Project Management JumpStart™
by Kim Heldman, PMP • ISBN: 0-7821-4214-1 • US $24.99

For those interested in beginning or exploring a career in project management, coverage includes:
- The basic skills of a project manager
- Creating project schedules and determining project budgets
- Communication and negotiation skills

### PMP®: Project Management Professional Study Guide, 2nd Edition
by Kim Heldman, PMP • ISBN: 0-7821-4323-7 • US $59.99

A comprehensive package to prepare for the PMP certification exam, this Study Guide provides:
- Detailed coverage of all PMP Exam Process Groups
- Refreshed content that make project management concepts clearer and easier to comprehend
- Companion CD with Testing Software, Flashcards for PCs, Pocket PCs, and Palm Handhelds, Two Bonus Practice Exams, and the Entire Book in PDF

### PMP®: Project Management Professional Workbook
by Claudia Baca, PMP; Patti Jansen, PMP • ISBN: 0-7821-4240-0 • US $34.99

A one-of-a-kind book that will give you hands-on experience as you prepare for the PMP exam, this workbook provides:
- Clear introductions that put the exercises in context and explain the importance of key project management skills
- Dozens of exercises designed by two veteran project managers to correlate directly with PMP objectives
- Cross references to the PMP Study Guide for additional instructional content

### PMP®: Final Exam Review
by Kim Heldman, PMP • ISBN: 0-7821-4324-5 • US $29.99

To ensure you're truly prepared for the exam, this book contains:
- Four complete practice tests
- Complex scenario questions with detailed explanations
- Companion CD with testing software and flashcards for PCs, Pocket PCs, and Palm Handhelds

### PMP®: Project Management Professional Certification Kit
by Kim Heldman, PMP; Claudia Baca, PMP; Patti Jansen, PMP
ISBN: 0-7821-4325-3 • US $109.97

A 3-in-one product, this kit includes:
- PMP®: Project Management Professional Study Guide, 2nd Edition
- PMP®: Project Management Professional Workbook
- PMP®: Final Exam Review

$124.97 Value
Save $15!

SYBEX®
www.sybex.com

# Sybex Covers CompTIA CERTIFICATION PROGRAMS

Sybex publishes self-study materials for the following CompTIA certifications:

- A+
- i-Net+
- IT Project+
- Linux+
- Network+
- Security+
- Server+

## STUDY GUIDES

- Practical, in-depth coverage of all exam objectives
- Includes hands-on exercises and hundreds of review questions
- CD includes a test engine, electronic flashcards for PCs, Pocket PCs, and Palm devices and a PDF version of the entire book

ISBN 0-7821-4244-3

## VIRTUAL LABS™

- Realistic, interactive simulations of key network features, such as router and switch functionality
- Step-by-step labs covering critical certification skills
- Customizable labs to meet your needs

ISBN 0-7821-4098-X

*In addition to being CAQC approved, Sybex is a cornerstone member of both the Security+ and Server+ Cornerstone Committee.*

ISBN 0-7821-3026-7

Go to **certification.sybex.com** for a complete listing of certification products

One Industry. One Voice.

## Sybex—The Leader in Certification

www.sybex.com

# TELL US WHAT YOU THINK!

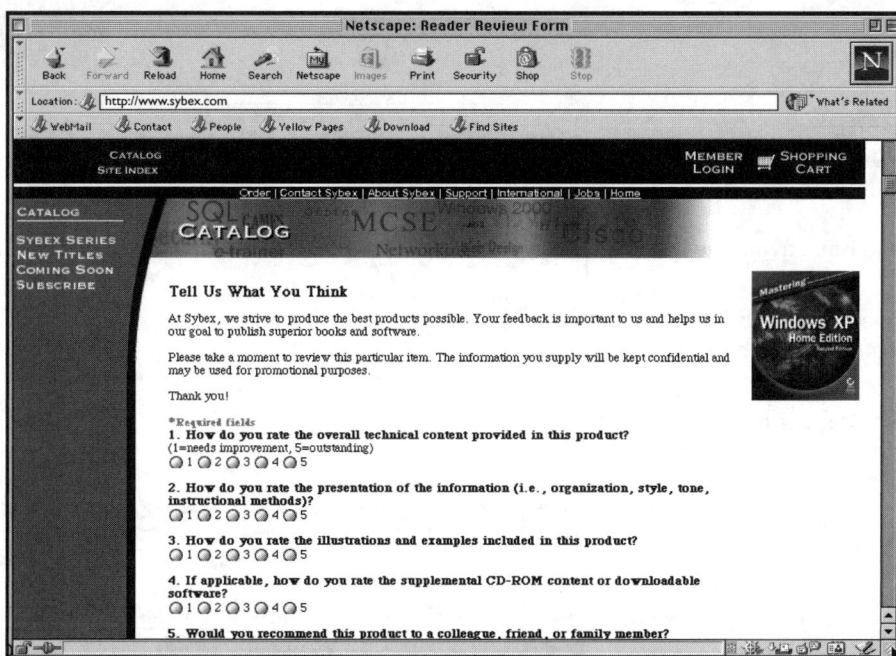

Your feedback is critical to our efforts to provide you with the best books and software on the market. Tell us what you think about the products you've purchased. It's simple:

1. Go to the Sybex website.
2. Find your book by typing the ISBN or title into the Search field.
3. Click on the book title when it appears.
4. Click **Submit a Review.**
5. Fill out the questionnaire and comments.
6. Click **Submit.**

With your feedback, we can continue to publish the highest quality computer books and software products that today's busy IT professionals deserve.

## www.sybex.com

SYBEX Inc. • 1151 Marina Village Parkway, Alameda, CA 94501 • 510-523-8233

# The Best PMP Exam Review Available!

*Prepare yourself for the PMP exam with hundreds of challenging sample test questions!*

- All four exams from the book available on the CD.
- Score your exam by topic area and find out what you need to study more before you take the exam.
- Supports question formats found on actual exam.

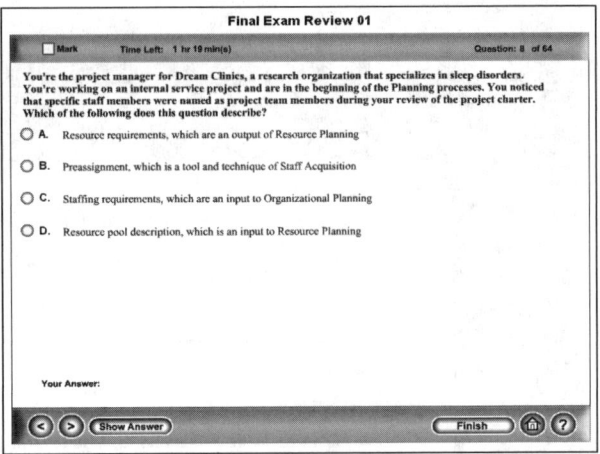

*Reinforce understanding of key topics with flashcards for your PC, Pocket PC, or Palm handheld!*

- Contains over 200 flashcard questions.
- Runs on multiple platforms for usability and portability.
- Quiz yourself anytime, anywhere!

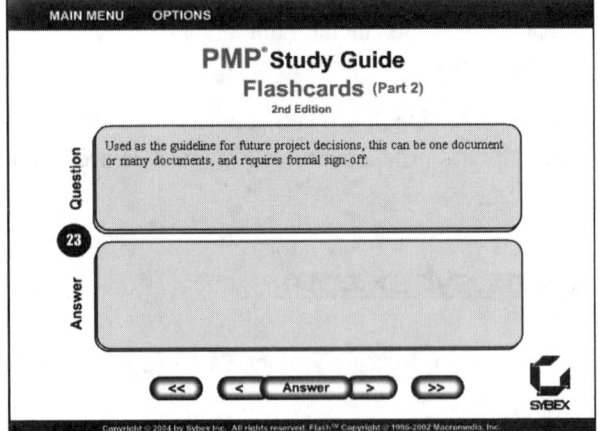